POCKET IMAGES

Stirling

The Bow at the turn of the twentieth century.

POCKET IMAGES

Stirling

Bob McCutcheon

NONSUCH

First published 1999
This new pocket edition 2007
Images unchanged from first edition

Nonsuch Publishing Limited
Cirencester Road, Chalford
Stroud, Gloucestershire, GL6 8PE
www.nonsuch-publishing.com

Nonsuch Publishing is an imprint of NPI Media Group

British Library Cataloguing in Publication Data.
A catalogue record for this book is available from the British Library.

ISBN 978-1-84588-428-4

Typesetting and origination by NPI Media Group
Printed in Great Britain

Contents

Dedication

John, one of the characters in recent years at the Top of the Town, used to sit outside his home in Spittal's House opposite Academy Road. For those of you who didn't know him, he had a film director's chair with the words 'Apprentice Millionaire' emblazoned on it. He always told Michael McDonald, another Top of the Town character, and myself that when he completed his apprenticeship and became a fully qualified millionaire he would take us on as apprentices. Sadly it was not to be. I always promised John that I would write another Stirling book just for him. Here it is.

Bob McCutcheon.

Introduction

Stirling, like all towns, has changed over the years since the advent of photography. Some of these were necessary changes which could lead to better living conditions and huge benefits to its citizens. In the one hundred and sixty years since the introduction of photography, Stirling has been linked to the railway, seen its first motor and had horrific traffic jams e.g. at the start of the Glasgow Fair in the days before motorway and other bypass routes. It has also been the scene of early aviation experiments as well as seen the demise of its trade by river. It has gone from telegraph communication to telephone to computer manufacture and communication. It has gone from a town where sewage and blood from slaughterhouses ran openly down the streets to accumulate in a foul smelling open pond at the bottom of the castle rock, to the headquarters of the major government office for the protection of the environment. It has gained a proper water supply, efficient fire fighting facilities and a proper free education system available to all of its children and the establishment of a local university, some departments of which are already world renowned. It has seen many of its industries founded, flourish and die. Stirling has been overshadowed by Falkirk in ironfounding but nevertheless Stirling ironfounders supplied structural cast iron for major buildings all over Scotland including Singer's huge sewing machine factory at Clydebank. Stirling was a major manufacturing centre for agricultural machinery as well as rubber and furniture. New industries have taken their place, although employment has dramatically changed not always to the advantage of the individual or the state.

It has seen improvement in housing for many of its residents and it has seen and, indeed was, at the forefront of the introduction of gas and electricity into universal usage.

Events over the last one hundred and fifty years have not always been sunshine and light. Armed conflicts and two World Wars have claimed the lives of countless numbers of Stirling's citizens. The military over the period has been a major part of the town's life. From being just another home posting for whatever regiment came its way, the Castle, the real *raison d'être* of Stirling's existence as the gateway to the Highlands, became the home of arguably Britain's most famous fighting regiment, the 91st and 93rd Princess Louise's Argyll and Sutherland Highlanders. The regimental museum is still in the Castle but recruits now no longer train there and the loss of other military links through the closure of the Admiralty Depot at Bandeath and the run down of the 'Government Stores' have had their effect. Many well known and historic buildings have been demolished or 'renovated' in a manner that sometimes verges on the criminal.

In our one hundred and sixty years, the residents have been involved in some of the major political events of the time and, although one wouldn't believe it, when one looks at the number who turn out to vote in local and national elections, there is universal franchise for all its citizens. This apathy on the part of the general public is something which disappoints me personally. Stirling's history is disappearing piece by piece, mainly at the hands of faceless local government officials, and soon it will be all gone. Whether it be the removal of the brass studs marking the site of the town's main medieval gate or the growing numbers of unnecessary pieces of street furniture or the wholesale vandalism of the area by the erection of architectural monstrosities such as can be seen at the bottom of Spittal Street or the crude vandalism in the renovation of historic buildings such as the town's Tolbooth, it must be discussed openly and people must speak up for the town and its historic past

In the following pages are a few images of Stirling's people, their surroundings and their life. Photography, the medium which has given us these images, is itself changing rapidly with the advance of digital technology where an image can be viewed on the camera and changed if desired before being computer enhanced and beamed across the world to another computer. Images from satellite cameras thousands of feet in the air can show up newspaper headlines. Will there be another generation of this type of book in fifty years time. I personally doubt it so enjoy the *Images of Scotland* series while you get the chance.

Bob McCutcheon, November 1999.

I HAVE JUST ARRIVED AT STIRLING

One

Streets and Buildings

We are at the bottom of Baker Street just about 1902 and these three early houses were soon to be demolished. The site is now occupied by the red sandstone block which houses the Italian restaurant and the Hot 'n Spicy takeaway as well as numerous flats. The one on the right was, at the time of the photograph, quite clearly marked as Refreshment Rooms. At the beginning of the nineteenth century it was the same and specialised in pies and porter. It was run by a Mrs Jaffray, whose husband was the town's letter carrier or postman. The post office at this time was at No.60 Baker Street and was run by William Paterson, a ropespinner and flax dresser. Jaffray later became the post carrier to Kippen and his place was taken by David Bell who used to carry the letters in a tin box suspended from his neck by a piece of cord. No junk mail then! It is reputed that the mail from London to Stirling could be held in one hand.

It is not Mr and Mrs Jaffray that we are interested in here, however, but rather their son, John, who left the town and moved to Birmingham. Here he did exceptionally well and was the founder of the Birmingham Joint Stock Bank and the Birmingham Daily Mail. He was present when his friend, the future King Edward, opened Birmingham's Infirmary, a ward of which was named after him. He was knighted for his public service and died in January 1901 not long before this photograph was taken. One part of the building still exists. A stone plaque which states 'Here I forebear my / Arms to fix / Lest me or mine should / Sell these stones and sticks' is in the Smith Art Gallery and Museum.

This is believed to be a hit at the Craigengelt family who owned the building next door. This is still in existence as 'Nicky Tams' public house. The arms of the Craigengelts can still be seen up above the door, although its old name of the Caledonian Vaults—which appeared during recent restoration—has now been painted over.

St Mary's Wynd, all of fourteen feet wide, photographed at the beginning of the twentieth century. We are looking into Broad Street and the tall building on the right beyond the ladies is the back of what is described and shown in another photograph as Rioch's Tavern. Note the pawnbroker's sign in the background. This belonged to Simpson the pawnbroker who had two or three shops in the area. The last pawnbroker in Stirling was Johnny Hill in Baker Street. One story told of him was that one of his regular customers was in the habit of pawning his Sunday best clothes and various other ornamental items every Monday morning. They were redeemed on Saturday evening for use on the Sabbath. This became such a habit that Johnny accepted the tied up bundle without opening it. One Monday, however, it did not feel quite right and he opened it after paying over the usual amount of cash to find that, for weeks, the customer had been pawning and redeeming an aged clootie dumpling. The gentleman in the foreground has his clay pipe in his mouth upside down as many smokers did then.

This picturesque little building is the Flesher's Tavern which once stood in St John Street. Even in the nineteenth century visitors to the town commented on its appearance. Lindley Sambourne, the artist, gives a sketch of it in *Our Holiday in the Highlands* by A. A'Beckett published about 1876. The artist was intrigued by a 'To Let' sign up in the garret. It was demolished in the 1950s clearances which were not all necessary and which cleared many of the town's historic buildings with their distinctive architecture. It will be interesting to see whether the buildings erected then to create an ersatz 'medieval skyline', as the architect put it, last even a fraction of the time that the original medieval and later skyline that he destroyed did. Already, sandstone blocks laid the wrong way are crumbling away to dust.

The Flesher's Tavern during demolition. Note the wall painting above the fireplace depicting the arrival of Mary, Queen of Scots, from France.

Looking down Broad Street to its junction with the Bow before the demolitions of the 1930s (centre of photograph) and the 1950s (right-hand side of photograph). The only building still left is the so-called Darnley house (the tall building on left of centre with the three dormer windows in the attic). Look above the centre window on the first floor and you will see a plaque which informs everyone that Lord Darnley lived there when he was out of favour with Mary, Queen of Scots. This story was put about by one of the Alexanders of Westerton at Bridge of Allan who was born there. He wanted to have been born somewhere special and he had the plaque fitted. Lord Darnley tended to live with Willie Bell, the town's treasurer, who lived and kept a public house further down the Bow.

Now occupied as the Highland Hotel, the main building in this view is that of the High School of Stirling. The schools in Stirling have a very ancient history but this complex of buildings only dates from the middle of the nineteenth century. Complex is the right word because, although today's lack of knowledge by officials who should know better imagines this as one, there are four separate buildings linked together. The Academy Road frontage (1854); the primary school at the Back Walk end of Academy Road (1907); the Elementary School (1887) inside the quadrangle and Spittal Street Wing (1888). The earliest part of the complex came about when an old pupil called Tovey Tennent, whose photograph is shown later, came to Stirling on a visit. He had made his fortune working for the East India Company and, seeing all the new buildings erected downhill, offered Stirling Council one thousand pounds towards a new school if they could decide within six weeks to build on this site.

At this time the site, as well as containing the writing school, the 1751 Trades Hall and the South Church building, was also the locus for the town's butchers who killed their livestock there. Indeed, a government report of the early 1840s describes blood and excrement being washed downhill into the mill dam, which was on the site of the Thistle Marches. The Council of the day (unlike today's) made up their mind very quickly and work commenced to designs by J.W. and J.M. Hay of Liverpool who actually envisaged a new school surrounding a quadrangle. Money became tight and it was not until the late 1880s that the Spittal Street wing shown here with its distinctive observatory was erected to designs by James Marjoribanks MacLaren. This former pupil unfortunately died before completion but he left one of the most imposing buildings of its day.

Right: Features of MacLaren's design were to be copied by others who are better known. Look at his lettering above the Observatory tower entrance. Think CRM. Think H as the back of a CRM ladderback chair. Think C and G turned on their side and you get the sweep of the arches in CRM's Hillhouse. Think windows at the Spittal Street end of Academy, once the conversion for art rooms, (now kitchens) and think of a simplified window for the Art School in Glasgow. Had MacLaren not died so young (aged thirty-seven), he would maybe have outshone the current hero of Scottish architecture.

Below: The photograph below shows the Rector's room in the school with its furniture and fixtures by McLaren and his partner, Robert Watson.

Baker Street or, as it was called previously, Baxter's Wynd. Although not bustling with people in the street this view, of about 1905, of the bottom half of this once thriving shopping area shows its influence as part of the town's life then. Many of the businesses shown here have closed and all have changed hands many times over. On the right can be seen the Star Hotel which had just been rebuilt in the 1890s. Note the occupants' names and businesses being advertised on the walls above the shops. The last of these business names to survive in this fashion was that of the Derby Bar (now Claymores) which still shone through repeated paintings until a few years ago when stone cleaning eventually removed this link with the past. The building on the extreme left was demolished to clear the McCulloch and Young site to enable the building of the 1960s concrete and glass block which houses various shops and office premises including the Inland Revenue. Note the wide expanse of cobbled roadway. Although there were contemporary complaints about noise from the iron bands on cart wheels rumbling over these cobbles everywhere within the towns it might be one of the solutions in historic towns like Stirling to car traffic by paving more streets with cobble setts as a means of slowing down traffic. The old time pavior laid these in a different manner to today with the cobbles bedded in with pitch poured into the joints. This prevented rainwater permeating to the underside of the cobble setts whereas today a dry cement mix is brushed in between. Quite often this shrinks when set and water is allowed to get in between.

Opposite top: We are at the foot of Broad Street looking towards St Mary's Wynd with, in the centre of the photograph, the Bruce Tavern. Where have all the good pub names of the past gone? The Bruce Tavern, The Wallace Arms, The Palace, The Cross Guns, The Stirling Arms, The Saracen's Head, The Red Lion, The Coffee House, The Bees Bink, The Caledonian Vaults, The Golden Grapes, The Guildry Arms, The Agricultural Arms, The Derby Bar, The Original, The Star, The Bush, etc. Answer: they have gone the same way as many of the good pubs – submerged in a sea of trendy rubbish by brewers and owners with no thought of history or locality or in many cases, of good taste. The building containing the Bruce Tavern was originally built as a house by the Forrester family of Logie possibly at the beginning of the sixteenth century. From 1777 to 1826 part of the top half of the building entered from St Mary's Wynd was the offices of the Stirling Banking Company. This bank, which issued notes in denominations of one guinea (one pound and five shillings), failed in July 1826. This was quite a difficult financial time for many of the smaller local banks and was compounded in the case of the Stirling Bank by rumours spread about by a disgruntled ex-employee. Within five years, however, the partners (sometimes at great personal sacrifice) had managed to pay all their creditors. The sense of duty and personal pride amongst Scots meant that very few of the Scottish banks which failed in the nineteenth century failed to satisfy creditors in full (and in very stark contrast to what happened in England).

This photograph shows the Bruce Tavern site cleared after demolition of the historic building in 1929.

This view from the palace in Stirling Castle comes from the start of the era of photography in Stirling. It was taken by Alexander Crowe, Stirling's first permanent photographer and the founder of a business, which lasted until the mid-twentieth century. There were travelling photographers before him but he made Stirling his home.

In 1826, Nicephore Niepce, who had been experimenting with various methods of producing lithographic plates by the action of light, met Louis Jacques Mande Daguerre. In 1828, a formal partnership was formed between the two men and this partnership was carried on by Niepce's son, Isidore, after the pioneer died. On 7 January 1839 the Secretary of the French Academy, Francis Arago, announced the 'Daguerreotype' process and on 19 August of the same year the French Government agreed to pay pensions to Isidore and Louis. In return the two men agreed to make a full disclosure of their process freely available to anyone. Five days before this one Miles Berry, an English patent agent, registered the process as patent 1839-1894. The result was that, initially, England was the only place in the world where royalties had to be paid. Like many others from the South of Britain he apparently believed that there was nothing beyond the Watford Gap or wherever and ignored Scotland. The result was that many fine English photographers came to Scotland to experiment and develop their craft. This meant that Scotland was at the forefront of this new medium.

Our man, Alexander Crowe, was a cabinet-maker from Kincardineshire. Having successfully constructed his own cameras and perfected the techniques, he travelled the country taking photographs for James Valentine of Dundee who was rapidly building up a business selling photographic views to the increasing number of tourists that the railways had brought to many areas. In 1859 he settled in Stirling and opened a small studio on the open ground behind the corner of Murray Place at the taxi rank. In 1872 he was joined by William Rodger who was soon made a partner and who actually ran most of the business after 1874. The firm of Crowe and Rodger produced many fine photographs during its existence. Unfortunately for our purpose these were mainly studio based but some of the early landscapes of Alexander are excellent records.

Look at this one. Photographed from the palace, it shows the Queen Anne garden in a very rough state instead of today's manicured lawns and the back of Snowdon House. Built in 1815 or so for the son of David Doig, the grammar school headmaster, this existed until 1922 when it was demolished to allow for the construction of Snowdon Cemetery. The frontage appears in many views of the Castle but not the back. In the background, very few houses appear in Victoria Square, Clarendon Place or indeed anywhere in the King's Park area. The cemeteries in Mar's Garden and the Valley are practically bare of stones having only recently been laid out. A fine, good quality view of the past.

Penny Millar's Slap runs down from the Castle Esplanade to the Ballengeich. One of its interesting characters in recent times was Harry Turbine, an attendant at the castle. This gave him the means to waylay castle visitors to his 'museum'. Three old pence was the admission price to Harry's house which was full of antiques (his words) or garbage (visitor's words) which had been acquired at Coull's Auction Rooms in the Craigs, where any lots not drawing a bid were knocked down to Harry. His uniform—peaked cap and black gabardine coat—was supplemented by a leather moneybag and a roll of tickets. Armed with these he would venture down to Station Road, which. at that time was a private road. Harry would approach unsuspecting motorists, show the roll of tickets and collect their 'parking charge'. After about ten or fifteen cars he would disappear .

Kirk Wynd was originally one of two narrow Wynds connecting Broad Street to the Holy Rude and to the ancient Manse which sat in St John Street. Dr John Moore, born in the manse, was an eighteenth-century literary figure, but tends to be overshadowed by his son, Sir John Moore. Sir John was a famous British Army General who died at Corunna in the Peninsular Wars, having managed to turn a potential destruction of the British Army into a fighting retreat which allowed a large part of the force escape by sea. Unfortunately, he was killed before the final stages of embarkation. 'Not a drum was heard, not a funeral note, / As his corpse to the rampart we hurried; / Not a soldier discharged his farewell shot / O'er the grave where our hero we buried.'

Looking down the bottom part of Spittal Street around 1900—a scene which has changed totally. The buildings on the right which jut out into the street were replaced by the present district court and by a now redundant police station in 1934. At the time of writing there are plans to relocate the court into the police office and possibly make the court available for a private police museum. At the time of this photograph these buildings were occupied by Sangster, a local china merchant, and by housing. The buildings on the left down to the first one gable end to the street were replaced in 1899-1901 with the current red sandstone block. Designed by McLuckie and Walter, whose office was at 15 Dumbarton Road, this block and the corresponding one in Baker Street were built for Lawsons Ltd, who were well known credit drapers. Lawsons' older premises in Baker Street were demolished in 1998 and are currently being developed as twenty-six flats for Forth Housing Association.

The next gable end building was demolished at the time of the First World War and the present building was erected as an auction hall in 1915. Designed by John Allan it, unfortunately, shows the lack of proper building materials during that period. The site has a chequered history with the building shown having in its time been home to the Stirling Journal newspaper when it opened in 1820, the meeting place for a religious sect known as The Bereans, the first home of the Salvation Army in the town, a leather dressing workshop run by one David Crocket, and a school. This latter was run during the 1860s by one Tammy Adams who had previously worked at Allan's School across the street. He closed his school and left to become a missionary in Glasgow! The small wall jutting out into the pavement beside the present building marks the building line shown here as the pavement is only 'on loan' to the local authority.

The small lane on the lower side of the present building has a sign saying 'Sma' Vennel'. This was put up by a private individual and is not the correct name for this link to Baker Street, its proper name is Dalgleish's Close. Named after one Peter Dalgleish who had a candle-making business there. The close which is on the extreme left of the photograph was called Wooley's Close after a proprietor of the Caledonian Vaults in Baker Street—a name, like many others of our historic pub names submerged in a sea of trendy, yuppie titles as 'Nicky Tams'.

This scene from the Second World War is an unusual view of the Castle in that it shows the Army Nissen Huts huddled down at the Haining. These were not ammunition huts as was claimed in a recent publication but were barracks for troops. Even before the troops moved out after the war these huts were being occupied by squatters desperate for housing. Local government rehoused some of these initial squatters but, with the full approval of national government, started a policy of demolition the instant that they were vacant. There was a large quantity of ammunition in the Carron and Endrick valleys above Kippen and throughout the Trossachs. Following a fatal explosion between Doune and Dunblane, this was hurriedly cleared. There were also poison gas shells stored against a possible invasion but these were in too bad a condition to move and were opened *in situ*. The result was that livestock on various farms throughout the area died or had to be destroyed. One argument put forward by the authorities that the gas was not the cause of this was that 'this gas was designed to kill humans not animals'!! A fine excuse showing that many officials think that the general public will believe anything that comes from an official source.

This fine photograph is by C. Bierstadt from Niagara in the state of New York and looks out from the castle area over Upper Castlehill towards the river and the Wallace Monument. The houses in the foreground have all been demolished. Their gardens have become part of the Ballengeich Cemetery. Orchard House Hospital, parts of which have only recently been demolished, can be clearly seen in the middle left. On the middle right Wallace Street and Union Street are not completed and there is no sign yet of Bruce Street. Round the old bridge on the left background we can see the rubber works, now replaced by John Forte student residences and the Forthbank Woollen Mill, which has now been replaced by a landscaped area. There is no Cornton and very little of Causewayhead.

No book on Stirling would be complete without some photographs of Stirling Castle. The first ones, however, are of a now forgotten view. The water in front is the flooded Raploch Quarry, one of many from which the town's building stone came. Flooded out in the last quarter of the nineteenth century it lay as a watery waste for many years before being drained and brought back into operation again. It flooded a second time, however, and was abandoned as a working quarry. Large unused holes in the ground are an asset to local authorities and it was pressed into service as a rubbish tip, was filled and grassed over to become the Quarry Park. It is now under the recent western by-pass and its initial roundabout next to the present fire station.

The other view, even older and taken closer to the Castle and Ballengeich, shows the houses on the slope, which have gone. Note that the slopes of the castle bear none of the trees and bushes, which have been allowed to grow up over the last twenty years.

Another view looking towards the Monument but this time taken from the Gowan Hills with the back of Albany Crescent (now demolished and with a carved stone taken from its frontage gracing the tabernacle of the Church of Jesus Christ Latter Day Saints in Salt Lake City, Utah). Still no Cornton building (that wouldn't come until 1947) and no Raploch at this end. Note the allotments on the left where Drip Road now starts and the more serious build up of Causewayhead Road from other photographs, such as that below.

The building shown here stood in Broad Street just about level with the Market Cross. It was known as Sir John Dineley's house, although from title deeds, it appears that this eighteenth century gentleman only owned part of the building. Sir John was the last member of an old English family with a rather tragic background. In 1741, his uncle, also Sir John, was on bad terms with his brother and heir, Samuel, because of a dispute over property. This brother was captain of the *Ruby*, a merchant ship, which at that time was anchored in the River Avon off Bristol. A mutual friend arranged a meeting between the two brothers in an attempt at reconciliation. This seemed to go well but as Sir John made his way he was kidnapped by Captain Samuel and six well-armed sailors. He was taken out to the *Ruby* and there, on the orders of his brother, he was strangled by two seamen called White and Mahoney.

The crime was discovered, Captain Samuel was executed and most of his estates and property were confiscated. His elder son, Edward, died insane twenty years later leaving our Sir John with the title and the remnants of the belongings of his parents. He had no real prospects of making money so he set out to do what many others, male and female, have done. He tried to marry money and, to this end, he advertised in the papers and issued handbills seeking a lady of means. He had no success in England and, moving to Scotland, he arrived in Stirling in 1768 and promptly bought this property in Broad Street. The building had been restored in 1715 but Sir John made his own alterations including creating what has been described as a roof garden complete with gooseberry bushes and fish pond on the gently sloping part of the roof but which, from the title deeds, appears actually to have been a balcony. Despite objections he managed to join the Guildry and recommenced his search for a bride with money. Sir John had sold this property before he left Stirling in 1771. He was to return for a number of years much later on, this time in very straitened circumstances, before leaving finally in 1792. He went to Windsor where he became one of the Military Knights who were pensioners kept by the State. Sir John died at Windsor in 1808, one of Stirling's more eccentric characters of the past.

These two photographs were taken from the top of the observatory tower of the old High School of Stirling and show various interesting buildings. On the right hand side of the first photograph can be seen some of the building work involved in constructing the red sandstone block of shops and flats which still stands at the foot of Baker Street. Originally built for Lawson's Limited the building shown is nearly complete with sheerlegs erected to assist in lifting the building materials onto the higher levels. The large roof running from left to right in behind the Dalgleish Court side of Baker Street was the roof of Drummond's Agricultural Museum. Within the memory of many inhabitants it was occupied by H.P. Watt, the auctioneer, and latterly by the Blewitt family, well known for their ability to cram all kinds of bric-a-brac, antiques and furniture into every available inch of space. A real life Aladdin's Cave. The other photograph shows the view down Spittal Street. On the left can be seen various buildings which have all been revamped into modern homes. A good example of this is the very first house where the former coachhouse and stable (true!) have been converted into part of a flat. Further down the street can be seen demolition work taking place as the site is prepared for the building of the present red sandstone block. This was built as an integral part of Lawson's building. When the demolition work was finished the site clearance was still not done as the site owners recouped part of their expense by selling off the 300 tons of excavated rock to the Town Council for use in road building.

The history of the occupancy of various church buildings is no less complicated than the history of the various Scottish religious sects. The history associated with this building is relatively simple. Until 1843 it belonged to the congregation of what was known as Old Light Seceeders under the Reverend William Mackray. He left and the church got sold to the congregation which was meeting in the Cowane's Hospital under the Reverend Alexander Leitch. It opened for business under this reverend gentleman on 26 November 1843. Now known as the South Free Church it served the congregation until 1902. In that year they moved to the North Free Church building in Murray Place. This then became the South Free Church. The congregation of the North Free Church moved to their new building, the Peter Memorial Church at Allanpark which is now called St Columba's. The South Free congregation eventually left the Murray Place building (which had been the North Free) and after lying empty for a number of years the building was taken over and renovated on behalf of the Baptist congregation who had sold their building on the opposite side of Murray Place so that the site could be incorporated into the Thistle Centre. If, gentle reader, you have followed all that we can go back to the photograph. The original Old Light Seceeders' building was bought in 1902 by the local authorities and incorporated into the High School complex. Many locals will remember it forty-to-fifty years ago as Domestic Sciences under Miss Brownlee and Biology under Mr Richardson upstairs while Mr Manson presided over the Technical Department downstairs. The building burnt down in 1960 and created even more overcrowding at the High School resulting in the move to new premises at Torbrex. The small house in the photograph was the Janitor's house and the gardens in front, part of the grounds of the 1751 Trades House, were built over when the Elementary and Primary Departments were constructed.

One long established feature of the Top of the Town which disappeared in 1935 was Henderson's the stationers and newsagents in the Bow. Alexander Henderson, who was a joiner and undertaker, took over the little shop at No.28 in 1865 when it had already been established for thirty years. Miss Isa Henderson, Alexander's daughter, was in charge when the business closed. One hundred years service to the community: not a claim that many businesses can make today. Our photograph shows old Alexander and Miss Isa at the door of the shop.

The Station Hotel in Murray Place was originally built as the Stirling Branch of the City of Glasgow Bank. This establishment failed spectacularly in the 1870s with many shareholders being reduced to penury and directors facing criminal charges. At the time of this photograph the hotel was being run by Mrs Lennox. The small lane at the side of the hotel on the right hand side of the photograph leads to the then Baptist Church hall. The first motor car seen in Stirling was in 1896 and was parked in the lane overnight. The local papers say how quietly and smoothly it left the sloping lane in the morning. The local papers cover this event in about half a dozen lines. Little did they know what a change it heralded! This was actually the overnight stop of the vehicle and its 'crew' on a momentous journey from Kelso to Perth. Some present day readers will maybe remember the little green hut which stood at the top of this lane. Offices for Jeffrey's Taxis, it was occupied for many years by an aged and very loquacious parrot. Another more relaxed age—his taxi was a Rolls Royce!

Barnton Street in the mid-1920s, again with very little traffic about. On the extreme right is the Post Office at the end of Murray Place. It was formally opened for business on Friday 24 May 1895 by Provost Kinross. The first letter was one from Provost Kinross to Henry Campbell-Bannerman the local MP thanking him for the help he had given the Council in getting the Post Office erected. He then sent off the first telegram which was to the Queen at Windsor. It read 'Provost and inhabitants of Stirling, opening new Post Office send this first telegram to wish Her Majesty many happy returns of her birthday.'

The building in the centre is, it will be noticed, built with curved rather than straight walls. There is a reason for this. The Episcopal Church in Scotland had severe restrictions placed on it during part of the latter half of the eighteenth century. One of these limited the number who could meet for a service at any one time. The congregation in Stirling, who, at that time, met in a building in the Lang Close between Broad Street and St Mary's Wynd got over this by erecting partitions which separated them into the legal number and their minister preached over the top. In 1792 these penal acts were removed and by this time they were meeting in the cellars of Glengarry Lodging. Looking at the front of this building today the small window on the right of the turnpike stair was once a doorway into the meeting room. Captain Sutherland, Stirling's first historian, states in his 1794 history of the town that the congregation had erected 'a very elegant place of worship' on this site. In 1845, they engaged John Henderson to design a new building on this site. This was to last the congregation until 1878 when they moved to their present building designed by Sir Robert Rowand Anderson in Dumbarton Road.

Their previous building in Barnton Street was bought by MacEwen Bros, a local grocery firm, who converted it for use as a grocery warehouse. The congregation, despite having sold the building, protested at this use which was to continue until 1880 when the building was demolished. The present buildings on the site utilize the church building site and the garden ground which was attached. Every inch of space was utilized, giving us the curved building shown above.

One building in the centre of the town currently being renovated and converted to housing is what began life as the Royal Hotel but will be better known to locals as one of the premises of the Stirling Co-operative Society. This imposing building is situated at the corner of Friar Street and Barnton Street. In August of 1840 Archibald Campbell, proprietor of the Royal Hotel at the bottom of Queen Street moved to his prestigious new premises. Archibald Campbell had been born in Killin and when he died at Upper Bridge Street in 1894 his remains were returned to his birthplace to be interred there. In November of 1904 the Stirling Co-operative Society, having acquired the premises applied for planning permission to convert the ground floor in to shops. The gentleman in the lum hat is Campbell himself and the photo is by Brown and Agnew of Dundee and Glasgow.

Although not a photograph with much action—indeed with no action at all—this nevertheless has one very interesting feature especially in the light of the 1995 revamp of Broad Street. Note the small standing stone to the right of the centre.

In 1792 the Town Council applied to the Court of Session for special permission to remove the Market Cross from the street as it was reputed to be in the way of traffic. Originally the Council wanted to have 'the great stair leading to the Council room and Tolbooth to be the Mercate Cross and place for publications in all time coming.'

However, one of the members of the Court—Lord Henderland—visited Stirling and suggested via the Court that the Town Council erect instead a pillar on the edge of the street. The council had no option and thus this pillar became officially the town's market cross. They were, however, allowed to adhere to part of their original plan. This was to place the 'town's arms', alias the unicorn, within the little niche, which can be seen as one descends the stairs of the Tolbooth. The unicorn or 'puggy' also spent some time adorning the entrance to the town's water reservoir in St John Street just above Academy Road.

It did, however, return to its place in the street when, under the pressure of Robert Yellowlees, the market cross was once more the subject of a petition to the Court of Session and permission was given to rebuild the cross in a new position.

During 1995 the market cross was again rebuilt. However, it was not returned either to its post-1891 position or to its pre-1792 position and, despite the involvement of such august partners of the Stirling Initiative, Stirling District Council and Historic Scotland, no petition appears to have been presented to the Court of Session. Does Stirling, having been one of the original four Royal Burghs in Scotland have an official spot on which proclamations, for example, of the death of a monarch and the accession of his or her successor, take place or does such an event have to be declared void? It would be interesting to know.

On a more down to earth theme note the Broad Street Brewery of James Duncan to the left of the Tolbooth. Previously in the ownership of one of the Burden family it was reputed by some to have produced a better class of beer a short time after funerals took place in the Holy Rude churchyard. A case of more body in the pint? Next door is the premises of Mrs Ging, the general dealer who is shown opposite with her donkey cart.

The scene at the unveiling of the rebuilt cross on 23 May 1891 is depicted in the lower photograph. In the centre can be seen Provost Yellowlees along with George Mowat and Dr Galbraith, two of Stirling's oldest inhabitants who have just unveiled the rebuilt Market Cross.

The date Saturday 12 January 1907 saw the unveiling of the South African War Memorial by the Duchess of Montrose. Designed by W. Hubert Paton, who was the nephew of Sir Noel Paton, and was cast by Messrs Singer & Sons of Frome in Somerset. Showing the figure of an Argyll at the engage, it bears the names of those who died including many local Territorials, officers of the 1st Battalion. The band and one hundred and forty men travelled up by special train from their then station at Chatham. They were met by pipers from the depot at the castle under Pipe Major Smith and marched through the town in full review order.

The 1st Battalion, 700 strong, was under the command of Duncan Campbell of Lochnell, saw its first action in South Africa in 1795 and was ordered out there on 5 May. In that campaign the battle of Wynburg and the taking of Saldanha Bay meant the defeat of the Dutch. The 1st Battalion of the now world famous Argyll and Sutherland Highlanders was originally raised as the 98th Regiment but this was changed to the 91st Argyllshire Highlanders while on this campaign. The Treaty of Amiens give the Cape of Good Hope back to the Dutch in 1803 and the battalion was the last British unit to leave. In 1835, most of the battalion (at this time stationed at St Helena) was posted back to the Cape. The three companies left behind provided the guard of honour at the disinternment of Napoleon and removal of his remains to France for reburial. From 1839 to 1855 the battalion, or its reserve battalion which was formed in 1842, served in South Africa. In 1842 the reserve battalion's troop ship, the *Abercrombie Robinson*, parted anchor cable and drifted aground. There were only two boats for the seven hundred aboard. Women and children were ferried ashore and lots were drawn for the disembarkation with the reserve being the last to leave the ship.

In 1848 the 1st Battalion came home while the reserve left to take part in the 1851-1853 Kaffir War. A draft of reinforcements for the reserve were aboard the *Birkenhead* which was wrecked on the African Coast in 1852. As on the previous episode with the *Abercrombie Robinson* the women and children were put ashore in the few small boats. The troops, to allow time for the small boats to get away, stood to attention on the deck as the ill-fated *Birkenhead* broke into pieces beneath their feet. The reserve came home to be absorbed into the 1st Battalion.

In June of 1858, twenty-nine officers and 285 men rode on donkeys across the Overland Route from the Mediterranean to the Red Sea on their way to India. In 1879, they were back in South Africa, under Lord Chelmsford fighting the Zulus after the military disaster at Isandlhwana. At the end of the Zulu Wars part of the Battalion went to Mauritius with part going to St Helena. During the Boer War the Battalion took part in some of the fiercest fighting of the war. This included actions at the Madder River, Maggesfontein and Paardeburg. Along with the regulars were one hundred and fifteen volunteers from the various volunteer detachments. Some of whom, as this monument testifies, never returned.

One of Stirling's disgraces. This is the house of John Cowane in a pre-1877 photograph
showing what the building looked like before a disastrous fire and partial demolition. John
Cowane was an early seventeenth century Stirling merchant trading both within Scotland and
to the Continent. As well as taking an active part in the affairs of the town while alive he left a
legacy which still has a major effect on today's town. His will meant the founding of Cowane's
Hospital which is beside the Holy Rude Church as a hospital for 'decayed Gild brethren'
although it never really spent much time through the centuries as that. As well as this lovely
little physical structure complete with its statue of John Cowane above the door (the statue's
right hand is wooden instead of stone) his will meant that money was available to invest.The
result was that Cowane's Hospital became a major feudal superior of the town. Income is still
being generated from buying and selling land, feu waivers and rent from farms and houses.
In 1921 the garden ground behind came on the market and it took more than six months to
decide whether to even buy it or not. There have been complaints for nearly one hundred years
about the local authorities not doing anything towards restoring this historic building. The
current proposals for restoration and usage were put forward fifteen years ago but this one-time
home of Stirling's greatest benefactor is still a ruin.

The Top of the Town in Stirling was a mass of closes and backlands and here we show a small selection of these. Most of them were swept away during the demolitions of the late 1920s and mid-1950s.

The Hangman's Close (left) ran through from St John Street to Broad Street. Note the portable ramp for rolling the barrels from Duncan's Brewery onto the delivery carts. The Coffee House (below left) was situated near the top of Baker Street just below the Bow. Its fame rested on the fact that this was the town headquarters of the Jacobite army during their siege of the Castle in 1746. The Long Close (below right) gave access to the Wynd from the middle of Broad Street.

The Church of Stirling

All Kind Thoughts

One sometimes wonders whether some of the early postcard manufacturers had a black sense of humour or whether they were totally unthinking. There are very few good vantage points for taking a view of the Holy Rude Church. This area is one but the graveyard tends to be there no matter what a photographer does. Nothing wrong with that but to add the words 'All Kind Regards', 'Happy Christmas', 'A Guid New Year' or even, as is on one beginning of the century card 'Wish you were here' is a bit much.

OLD GRAVE-STONE IN STIRLING CEMETERY
The original name was cut out, and the present one substituted, in 1866. This epitaph is found, with variations, in different churchyards in the British Isles, attributed to Bishop Henshaw of Peterborough, 1679. (See Benham's "Quotations," published by Cassells.)

33

Opposite page: Three photographs by Alexander Crowe show, above, the Martyr's Monument and, below these, the statuary group below the Ladies' Rock. During the 1850s, due largely to the efforts of Revd Dr Charles Rogers, chaplain at the castle, the town's ancient churchyard at the Holy Rude was extended. The old wall round the Church was removed—at night by the fairies as the local newspapers put it—and Mar's garden (behind Mar's Wark) and the Valley —scene of horsefairs and tinker encampments—incorporated. A plan was drawn up by the Edinburgh architects, Peddie and Kinnear, and walks and grassed areas for lairs constructed. Some of the money was raised by public subscription but a substantial proportion was given by William Drummond, the local seed merchant, who is himself buried near the Salem Rock pyramid which he had erected. The initial view of the Martyrs' Monument shows it shortly after it was erected in 1859. The second shows it shortly afterwards when the cupola was erected to protect the marble statues from the elements. The lamb was removed in the 1890s. Contrary to popular belief the group is meant to commemorate the martyrdom of the larger of the two females. She was Margaret Wilson, daughter of Gilbert Wilson of Glenvernock in Penningham parish in Wigtonshire. Although their parents were Episcopalian, the two girls (the smaller figure is Agnes) and their brother were Covenanters. They spent many months hiding in the wilds of Wigtownshire but after the restoration of the monarchy in the shape of Charles II, the laws against Covenanters was relaxed slightly and the trio came out of hiding. While visiting Agnes McLauchlan or Lauchlison, the wife of Gilbert Mulligan or Millikin, a carpenter in Kirkinner, they were betrayed by one Patrick Stuart. They, like everyone else over the age of sixteen, had to take the 'Abjuration Oath' giving up the Presbyterian religion. Refusing to do so they were tried and sentenced to death. The charge was High Treason and amongst the accusations levelled at them was that they had fought at the Battle of Bothwell Bridge. This had taken place when the Wilson girls were children and Margaret McLauchlan was over 65! The verdict was guilty but Gilbert was allowed to ransom the young Agnes for £200. So much for the high minded principles of the authorities. The two Margarets were, however, sentenced to be drowned on the Solway estuary. A petition was raised and a reprieve was granted by the Privy Council but eleven days after this happened in Edinburgh the authorities in Wigtownshire carried out the death sentence.

On 11 May 1685 the two Margarets were tied to stakes in the fast-incoming tide of the Solway. The elder woman was soon swept away and drowned but young Margaret survived longer. She was untied and asked to take the oath. Refusing, she was again tied to the stake and was soon engulfed in the rising tide. As the waters covered her she could be heard singing the 25th Psalm.

Let not the errors of my youth
Nor sins remembered be;
In mercy for the goodness' sake,
O Lord, remember me.

Today the monument to this brave girl is in a terrible state with glass broken, heads missing and marble weathered. Another indictment on a council who supposedly wish to encourage tourists to this beautiful town but only contemplate the grandiose schemes and ignore its true history and its once beautiful features.

In 1985 an open-air service was held in the graveyard to commemorate the drowning of the two Margarets. This was the first service to be held there since the days of Ebenezer Erskine. The collection that day was to go towards the restoration—an offer that the local council refused to take up—on the basis that they did not approve of the speakers.

One well known business in Stirling until recently was that of Graham & Morton. Founded in 1830 by a local man, William Graham, in Baker Street the business soon expanded to new premises in King Street. In 1844 David Morton came as an assistant but by 1861 he was a partner. Over the years the business, which had started purely as an ironmongers, branched out into ironmongery and furniture manufacture, interior design, and a myriad of other ventures. They could certainly live up to their designation of 'Complete House Furnishers'. The photograph above shows the frontage of their shop in Dumbarton Road at the beginning of the twentieth century. As well as the Dumbarton Road premises, the firm also had at this time a huge factory in the Burghmuir (below) and premises in King Street and in Falkirk.

Friar Street or, as it was known earlier, Friar's Wynd about the beginning of the twentieth century. Note Dale the hairdresser and perfumery and the telephone exchange sign. The National Telephone Company brought the phone to Stirling in 1886. There were two numbers initially in the town. One was the Golden Lion Hotel and one was Johnstone's, the fish merchant, in Port Street. This soon expanded to various other businesses and homes and, despite some opposition because of wires being trailed through trees etc., the phone came into widespread usage. Most homes did not, however, have one and we reap the benefit of the early days. Until 1916 there were three postal deliveries per day in Stirling and the postcard was the local telephone call of the time. A Stirling resident could send a card to a friend in Glasgow early in the morning, have the card delivered and the friend waiting at the station in Glasgow for their arrival on a train from Stirling at lunchtime. Postcards were produced and sent in vast numbers and collections made then now provide many of the views and events found in books like this.

One of the premier vantage points in Stirling is the top of the tower at the Holy Rude Church. This, however, is not a spot that can be visited by the public. This is a poor substitute—a view of the esplanade from the tower of the church. Over the years of the twentieth century various changes have taken place on the Esplanade. The 75th Stirlingshire Regiment has been moved from the bottom of the steps at the Pithy Mary to the Esplanade; the South African Monument erected; what is now Tourist Board offices converted from housing to hotel and now visitor centre; the old Militia Stores building near the portcullis demolished; the railings removed from around the Bruce statue; and, of course, the actual surface change from cobbles to grass to tarmac. The building at the junction was renewed at various times and now all structures have gone completely to give way to a landscaped area. One feature that existed in this area and is now gone was the Palace Gardens and Tea Rooms.

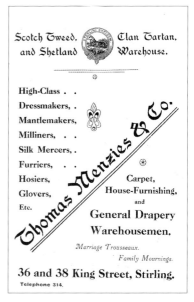

Scotch Tweed. and Shetland

Clan Tartan. Warehouse.

High-Class . .
Dressmakers, .
Mantlemakers,
Milliners, . .
Silk Mercers, .
Furriers, . . .
Hosiers,
Glovers,
Etc.

Carpet,
House-Furnishing,
and
General Drapery
Warehousemen.

Thomas Menzies & Co.

Marriage Trousseaux.
Family Mournings.

36 and 38 King Street, Stirling.
Telephone 314.

One of the more distinctive buildings in this view of the top of King Street is that of Thomas Menzies & Co. with its oval windows on the top floor. This drapery business was founded in 1861 by two partners and traded under the name of Menzies and Melrose. After about three years they purchased various old properties at the top of King Street and built the large shop premises shown here. They later bought a drapery business in Peebles and, eventually, Mr Melrose took over that for himself and left Stirling solely to Thomas Menzies. He had come originally from Blackford and learnt his trade in Paisley. After a spell in Stirling he went to Manchester where he met his future partner. It is interesting to note that, in these days of recent legislation relating to the working week, that Menzies were one of the first shops in the town to close at the then unheard of hour of five o'clock on a Saturday. Until they and a few other businesses did this shops in Stirling stayed open until eight or nine o'clock at night and sometimes later. Some did not close on a Saturday evening until nearly midnight. Having said that we find now that national and international retail concerns in the town are open late every Thursday and all day every Sunday. There is even a planning application lodged to open the Tesco superstore twenty four hours a day. As these large retail outlets rely heavily on part-time staff they can sustain this level where the small family run business can not fall in with changed shopping patterns. Many of these small businesses are already open to the public six days and, for a variety of reasons, also work Sundays. These large concerns, most of which take their profit out of area, are feted by local authorities at the expense of the small trader. The authorities forget that these large companies can just as easily up sticks and go. In the meantime, the small diversified shop closes and without diversification, the town can not compete and dies.

The drapery business that Thomas Menzies served his apprenticeship in has changed out of recognition. He had a limited range of materials and great difficulty in finding out the latest fashions. He had to provide a very professional, personal service with each item sold being exactly what the customer wanted in material, colour, style and fitting even if instant tailoring was required.

Bishop Gleig's house still stands in Upper Bridge Street, one of the fine Georgian and early Victorian houses that grace one side of the street. Bishop George Gleig came from an old Jacobite family from the north east of Scotland. He attended Aberdeen University from the age of thirteen and left with a brilliant scholastic record. He came to Stirling in 1787 after a number of years at Crail and was here for fifty-two years. After living in Baker's Wynd (now Baker Street) in the house shown here, he moved to Upper Bridge Street. He was created Bishop of Brechin in 1808 and Primus of the Episcopalian Church in Scotland in 1816. He superintended the compilation of the third edition of the *Encyclopaedia Britannica* and contributed various articles including the entry on Theology and the one on Metaphysics. A large stone used to stand beyond the Old Bridge on the way out to Causewayhead. As an old man, his daily exercise was to walk as far as this stone where he would rest before returning home. This stone, known as the Bishop's Stone, was consigned to Polmaise rubbish tip by Stirling Council workmen within the last two years. Bishop Gleig, in his final years was too frail even for this walk, and he died on 9 March 1840 near the end of his eighty-seventh year. One of his sons, George Robert Gleig, was born in Stirling in Baker Street in 1796. After serving as a soldier in the Peninsular Wars and in the American Wars of 1812-1814 he completed his religious studies. After a period at Ivy Church in Kent, he became the Chaplain of Chelsea Hospital and, after two years there, he was appointed Chaplain-General of the Forces in 1846. As well as re-organizing that Department he wrote extensively— historical novels and religious, historical and biographical works.

The Athenaeum at the top of King Street is generally just called the Steeple. King Street itself was, until the 1840s, called Quality Street. The Steeple was built as shops, town's offices and reading rooms in the 1814-1816 period. Built to a design by local architect Allan Johnstone, who was responsible for most of the design and building of Queen Street, it is quite a delicate structure. This view does not show its fine lines off to advantage because the frontage is now dominated by the heavy portico supporting the statue of William Wallace. This statue is by the sculptor Handyside Ritchie and, although a good piece of work, caused great disagreement in the town when it was bought. Dr Charles Rogers was apparently in Ritchie's studio at the time that initial fundraising was being organized for the erection of the National Wallace Monument. He saw the statue of Wallace, liked it and bought it even although he had no money. He then approached the council seeking cash and a place to erect it. Nobody wanted anything to do with it and William Drummond, the local seedsman, paid for it and had it delivered to Rockdale, his home on the Cambusbarron road. Attitudes suddenly changed from Rogers being statue mad to 'this is a fine piece of sculpture' and where there had been derogatory comments about location such as 'it's another stone so put it in the quarry in Barnton Street' to efforts to place it in a prominent place. Rogers set up a subscription to erect a plinth and initially an attempt was made, by blocking off a section of King Street (in the middle of the road just about level with the entrance to the later Arcade). This, however, interfered greatly with the traffic and the current site was chosen. A public subscription was raised and this portico erected. Despite attempts to lighten its appearance by filling in the window behind and carving tracery on its surface, it is still too clubby for the rest of the building. Nevertheless, the council of the day deserves praise for changing their mind and supporting its erection and leaving us with such a significant feature.

This corner of Murray Place is one street scene that has changed almost out of recognition. This photograph is from about 1905 while the bottom one is 1924. On the left side the low building next to the Arcade has been transformed. On the right hand side the North Church (extreme right), the Baptist Church (with cupola spire) and the Station Hotel have been demolished as part of the Thistle Centre clearances. They have been replaced by a 'masterpiece' of some modern architect's twisted imagination which looks like a Legoland model. The building beyond the Station Hotel and on the other side of the Station road was home to the County club. It has been replaced by a concrete and glass shop and office building which is, if anything, worse. The carriages lined up on the right were based at the Station Hotel and were the then equivalent of the smart white modern taxis which now sit on the other side of the road.

The town's own generating plant was housed in the red brick building which still exists in Colquhoun Street. It was a coal-fired power plant with four Lancashire boilers 28ft by 6ft supplying steam to various engines manufactured by Messrs Allan and by Bellis & Morcomb. These drove the generators made by Mather & Platt and by Siemens. They gave sterling service in the early years of the town's move into the modern world.

Opposite bottom: Although not a particularly good photograph this is a very historic one for the town. It shows the first use of the town's electricity system. It was taken on the evening of 1 March 1900. That morning word had been received that a British force under the command of Lord Roberts had relieved the town of Ladysmith, which had been besieged by a large force of Boers. The Town Council, acting at a speed almost unheard of today, had an emergency meeting that morning; organised an early closing for shops; a fireworks display and bonfire on the Gowan Hills and the illuminations shown above. The town's electricity supply was almost due to go into operation and they brought the official opening forward to that evening. A supply powering a line of bulbs was strung from the scaffolding being used to what was then a new building for the Clydesdale Bank (now the Ginger Bar and Cafe) to the Town Council offices which were then located in the Steeple and across to the opposite side of the street. The panel across the Steeple itself carries the name 'Roberts' in capital letters. As can be seen there were also lines of bunting. A few minutes after this photograph was taken the new electric street lamps in King Street were switched on to herald a bright start to the twentieth century for the thousands crammed into the street.

Stirling's only surviving newspaper from last century is the *Stirling Observer*. Founded in 1836 by Ebenezer Johnstone it occupies premises in the Craigs. These have just been refurbished and newly painted and are a far cry from Ebenezer's first premises in Baker Street. The Craigs and the corner of Port Street were revamped from the 1870s to the beginning of this century and our top photograph shows the last of the early cottages which lined the south side of the street. It is basically on part of this site that the current *Observer* building stands. The *Observer* newspaper itself, which is quite often described as the 'Stirling Rag' (which is usually a term of endearment rather than disparagement), has just moved from its familiar broadsheet of the last one hundred and sixty years to a modern tabloid format. In a photographic book about Stirling it is perhaps relevant to note that the earliest surviving photograph known to be taken in Stirling is of Ebenezer's daughter, Janet Graham Johnstone, taken just before she died in 1843. As someone who obviously supported the new technology of the time, I'm sure Ebenezer would approve of today's newspaper production.

The top picture shows a busy scene in the sidings of Stirling Railway station in the 1920s. The company some of whose activities are depicted here is actually Wordie & Company who were railway contractors organizing warehousing, transportation and distribution via the railways throughout Britain and Ireland. Here they have been driving in hay for carriage by rail. Hay was (and still is) a major agricultural product from the carse land about Stirling. Ryegrass is grown for animal consumption while timothy is grown both for consumption and for harvesting for seed. Yields for seed from the carse are among the highest in the world for quality and quantity. Up to the time of this photograph the demand for hay for feeding the vast numbers of horses being used for commercial purposes in the towns and cities of Britain was almost insatiable. This demand started to wane after the end of the First World War as the natural process of the spread of new technology in the shape of motor vans and lorries was speeded up considerably when the government started selling off surplus vehicles.

Wordie & Co. themselves had vast numbers of horses but they too modernized and shown in the lower picture, although not photographed in Stirling, is their first steam wagon.

The scene is the corner of the Craigs and Cameronian Street where the Norman McEwan Centre now stands and the building is the old Craigs Free Church. The tender for doing the building work was accepted on 4 June 1783 with a promised finishing date agreed by the builder—one Robert Taylor—of 1 October 1783. His bill for the stonework—walls of freestone, a hefty 2ft 6in thick—was the princely sum of just over £61 while John Gibbons and Archibald Telford supplied the roof and seats for £120. In total with plasterwork and metalwork the bill for this plain but substantial building came to just over £284. The wall in the photograph was built the following year for nearly £8 while the session house shown at the far end was built about two years after. The Reformed Presbyterian Congregation had to borrow a certain amount of money to pay off these seemingly small sums but one thing to bear in mind is that the wages of that period were much lower than today. In fact, the wages for one of the stonemasons working on the building amounted to 1s 2d per day (6 pence). The first minister of the new church was John MacMillan who was ordained at Stirling in 1778 and died in 1819 to be buried in the Holy Rude graveyard. When he came to Stirling at first he apparently stayed in Bothwell Hall at the top of St John Street but in 1874 he bought four acres just outside the town, where he built a largish house, byre and stable. His buildings have long gone to be replaced by a fine mansion house for Peter Drummond of the Stirling seed firm. This mansion was substantially extended in 1928 to become headquarters for Stirling County Council.

But back to the Reverend gentleman. He was to become the first Moderator of the reformed Presbyterian Church in Scotland and, if that did not keep him busy, he ran a special training class in Stirling for aspiring ministers. Young men came from all over the West of Scotland and Ireland to the training college in the little session house beside the Craigs Church. After the death of John MacMillan it took the congregation eight years to find someone to replace him. The Reverend William Stevenson came to the church in 1827 and was to remain until 1848 when he moved to Dundee and then to Melbourne, Australia. One important step taken by the congregation in 1843 was the construction of a manse—No 6 Albert Place—for their minister.

The church has gone, as have all the older buildings down that part of the Craigs but the building of the stonework by Robert Taylor for £61 back in 1783 certainly gave value for money.

The Cameronian Kirk was demolished in 1935 but the site still served a useful purpose with the opening in October 1937 of the Craigs Fellowship Hall which was built for the congregation of St Columba's at a cost of £2,200. A far cry from Robert Taylor's £61.

Two

People and Events

Matron's rounds, Stirling Royal Infirmary.

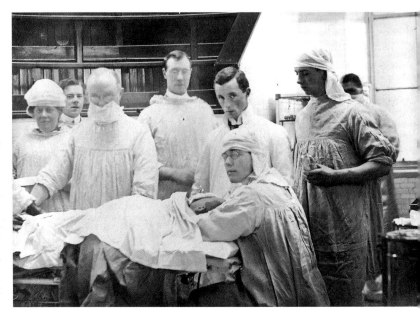

Stirling Royal Infirmary around the time of the First World War. The present Infirmary was opened in 1928 but before that it was located in Spittal Street in the building now occupied by Forth Valley Health Board. Originally the central part was built as the local branch of the Commercial Bank in 1826-1827. They vacated the premises in 1872 and it became the Stirling Infirmary in 1874. The town had had a dispensary but it had ceased operation in 1851 and there was a crying need for a facility of some description. Mainly due to the efforts of Thomas Muir, a local coal merchant, funds were raised and a site sought. Many other groups were looking for a similar sized site for the Smith and for a new courthouse and this led to a certain delay. However the new infirmary was officially opened on 10 June 1874 and on 23 November the organizing committee received word from Queen Victoria that the building could be called the Royal Infirmary of Stirling. As need grew the building was extended at various times and in 1906 a new convalescent home was opened at Chartershall near Whins of Milton.

The first proposals for such a facility had come with an offer from an anonymous donor to give a substantial amount towards the building costs on condition that it be called the Queen Victoria Convalescent Home. It was meant to mark the monarch's Diamond Jubilee in 1897. It was not, however, until 1902 that adverts appeared in the local press looking for householders willing to take in convalescent patients. This was successful and money was raised to build a new building. About £3,000 was raised and the anonymous donor stepped in again bringing his contribution to £5,000.

This photograph shows an operation about to start. Note the chloroform pad over the patient's mouth and nose and the assistant with the bottle of chloroform. No need to ask this subject to be still for the photographer!

Here the staff of Spittal Street are waiting in front of the building for King George V and Queen Mary passing en route to the Castle in July 1914. By the 1920s the population of the town had risen rapidly mainly due to the expansion of the coal mining industry locally. There had also been pressure on the facility during the First World War when 2,613 servicemen were treated for various injuries. The Spittal Street building was incapable of any more expansion and a new site was sought. Ground at Livilands was bought and James Miller, whose practice was in Glasgow but who stayed in Randolph Road beside the new site, was engaged as architect. The work started in June of 1926 and the new infirmary was ready for its official opening on 10 August 1928.

Wars make money for the companies producing the weapons, ammunition, clothing, equipment, etc., but they also involve Government in spending money on a vast scale. During the First World War the British Government naturally raised cash by clawing back the people's cash by encouraging National Savings and by the sale of War Bonds. After the tank made its first appearance on the battlefield on 15 September 1917 it was to many civilians a mythical creature capable of anything and how better to attract public attention than by sending some round the country as fundraisers. The 'capable of anything' belief was actually misplaced as in the first actions, the tanks were not always ready to go, broke down, lagged behind the infantry, got lost and, in many ways, were a failure. They did, however, frighten the enemy in many cases. One German is quoted as complaining that it was 'not war but bloody butchery'—an interesting philosophical point. They also improved greatly over the years and became a lethal fighting machine. Our photograph shows His Majesty's Landship *Julian* fundraising outside the Municipal Buildings on 8 August 1918.

Opposite bottom: Stirling Burgh Police Football Club—Season 1913/14. The caption to this photograph by Norman Craig says it all. One thing to note—there is not a panda car in sight. These fellows are from the days when policemen (of all ranks!) actually walked a beat in Stirling on a regular basis. One claim to fame that the Old Burgh Police Force had was that it was believed to be the first Force to apprehend a criminal using the telegraph. This occurred when a criminal stole a pair of blankets in Stirling and then got onto the Glasgow train. A signal was tapped out along the wires and the Glasgow polis met him at the railway station for a prompt return to Stirling.

What the well-dressed postie wore in Stirling during the latter years of the First World War—one aspect of which was the taking over of many male-orientated jobs by the 'weaker' sex. This included delivering the mail. These two young ladies joined the Post Office staff at Stirling. Do you know who they are?

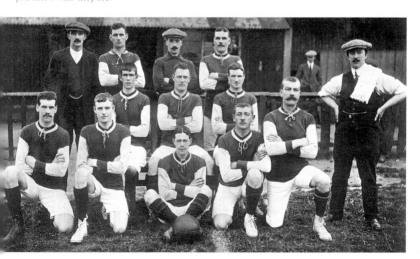

The Salvation Army's first meeting place in Stirling was in David Crocket, the leather dresser's workshop in Spittal Street. They later moved to what is now The Coffee Shop in the same street but, by the 1920s, they had obtained ground in Irvine Place on which to build a new citadel. On Saturday 16 July 1921 Commissioner and Mrs Jeffries and Brigadier and Mrs Parkin came to Stirling to participate in a flag-hoisting ceremony on this site. These photographs show parts of the crowd on this memorable day for the local unit. The citadel has itself been abandoned in favour of a new citadel in the Raploch and a housing development has been built on this Irvine Place site. Note the advertising hoardings on the opposite side of the street shown in the photograph below. The Picture House cinema—now demolished and under part of the north end of the Thistle Centre—was showing *The Pride of the North*. This was the story of a Yorkshire mining village. Another attraction advertised is the Scenic Railway at the local Bridge of Allan Highland Games.

Most people in the area did not know until recently that Stirling has a long association with aviation. John Damien, a French monk, attempted to fly from the Castle walls to Paris. Unfortunately for him, his wings were made of hen feathers instead of the eagle feathers which he said later he should have used, and he plunged to the ground. This was in 1507 and another intrepid aviator in the area was taking to the air in his gas filled balloon in 1831. Charles Green hoped to use the town's gas works but it was too small and so he took off from Alloa instead. As far as actual powered flight was concerned two locally based men were involved in early experiments and both went on to higher things (no pun intended). Harold and Frank Barnwell were among the founders of Grampian Engineering Company Ltd and were passionately interested in powered flight. Frank was the designer and Harold was the pilot. They constructed a number of aeroplanes with varying degrees of success eventually winning the J.R.K. Law prize for the first Scottish aeroplane to fly more than half a mile. Frank went on to become chief designer with the Bristol Aeroplane Co. and designed such aircraft as the Bulldog, Beaufighter and the Blenheim (one of which recently did a flypast over Stirling). He was killed test flying a small private plane he had designed. Harold became chief test pilot for Vickers and was killed on a flight during the First World War.

This photograph is of the Great Daily Mail round Britain air race in 1911. Up the East Coast from London to Stirling and back to London via the West Coast for a prize of £10,000. The first man to land at Stirling's King's Park was a Frenchman by the name of Andre Beaumont, a pseudonym as he was a member of the French armed forces, while another Frenchman Jules Vendrine was second and the third was J. Valentine who was the first British pilot. The Barnwells helped at the King's Park with supervising the entrants and the local scouts helped guard the planes from the public. The photograph shows No.24, the aeroplane belonging to Gustav Hamel, who was later lost somewhere in the English Channel. (On page 54 is the aeroplane of Andre Beaumont.can be seen.)

Valentine had a spot of trouble on his next leg of the race when he descended down through the rain to see where he was. He had reached Castlecary but he had also reached near zero altitude and flew into a hedge, damaging his propeller. He had to return to Stirling by train and wait for a new one to be sent from Carlisle. All in a day's work for 'those magnificent men in their flying machines'.

Jules Vendrine was a well-known distance and air display pilot and became famous on both sides of the Channel flying his plane *La Vache*.

A First World War ploughing scene on King's Park Home Farm.

The largest event in the farming year in Scotland is the Royal Highland Show held at Ingliston, near Edinburgh. Until the Royal Highland & Agricultural Society acquired this permanent site in fairly recent times, this annual show was held in a different venue every year. Stirling was a popular choice and, indeed, the coming of the show in 1872 forced the Caledonian Railway to erect a footbridge between platforms as hosts of visitors complained. This photograph is of the stand belonging to the Gourock Rope Company Ltd. at the fifth show held in Stirling. The first was in 1833 but this photograph was taken nearly a century later in July of 1921. One of their posters advertises 'Birkmyre' cloth suitable for tarpaulins for binders and motor tractors. There were not many of the latter in the Stirling area. Indeed, only about fifty Fordsons and a sprinkling of other makes, such as Case, had been sold in this area over the previous four years. The stand displays a variety of ropes and twines with bags of binder twine standing upon the right. The introduction of the knotting device which transformed a reaper (which left the crop lying on the ground to be gathered and tied by hand into sheaves) into a binder which elevated the crop by means of canvas elevators in through a mechanism which tied a twine round the sheaf in 1879 was a major step forward in agriculture. Nowadays, very few binders remain in working condition and are mainly in the hands of vintage enthusiasts with giant combine harvesters being the implement commonly seen in the harvest fields.

The salesman on the left has on boots and gaiters, which were a necessity this particular year. The park was newly seeded after being partly ploughed up as part of the war effort in 1917 and due to the very inclement weather was quickly churned up. Indeed, if it had not been for the liberal use of bark laid up and down the roads between the stands the show would have to have been abandoned.

The Alhambra Theatre had a film programme to coincide with the show. *Cultivation and Courtship* or *A Tractor to Attract Her* was a two reel love story about a dashing young farmer who was in favour of modern mechanisation and his attempts to persuade his lady love's father, who was in favour of horses and well established methods, that he was a suitable catch. This 'entertaining and educational' film was produced by Agricultural and General Engineers, Kingsway, London. They were the first company to use the cinema in such a way, combining a 'very interesting and attractively produced love story with an ingenious introduction to some of the specialities of the thirteen or fourteen well known manufacturers who make up the company'. They don't make them like they used to do!

Stirling's Member of Parliament for many years was Sir Henry Campbell-Bannerman. His service was recognized by the erection of a fine statue near the bottom of the Back Walk. This photograph is not of the statue itself but of the macquette and, although the statue bears the words 'An Empire's tribute' not as much work was expended on the finished article as was intended. The macquette shows a lot more decorative detail. Despite his family coming from the Thornhill area, Sir Henry made his Scottish home in Perthshire and when he died in 1908 he was buried in Meigle churchyard. One little known distinction that Sir Henry had was that he was the first person to have the official title of Prime Minister. Those who went before him had the official title of First Lord of the Treasury. He represented the Stirling District of Burghs from 1868-1908.

IN MEMORY OF THE LATE RT. HON. SIR H. CAMPBELL-BANNERMAN

ONE OF BRITAIN'S GREATEST STATESMEN

THE LATE PRIME MINISTER

"HOUSES OF PARLIAMENT

No. 10, DOWNING STREET

These four cards by Stirling photographer Mark Bennet tell their own story. These are the first four drives off the first tee of the newly extended course of Stirling Golf Club. There is the possibility that golf was played in the King's Park but the Stirling Club was formed in 1869 when seventy-two locals formed the Club with a seven green course. Twenty years later a number of local tradesmen formed another club known as Stirling Victoria. They erected another makeshift clubhouse behind the earlier club's more substantial premises on the site of the present No.30 Victoria Place. The two clubs remained separate entities until 1953.

3.

OPENING OF EXTENDED COURSE
STIRLING GOLF CLUB   JUNE 29.1912.

The Stirling Ladies Golf Club was formed at the turn of the century. In 1901, the seventy-eight members built a small clubhouse beside the other two in Victoria Place. Again it remained a separate entity until the mid-1950s. The original seven hole course was extended to nine holes in 1877 and in 1911 the club applied to the Commissioner of HM Woods and Forests (the actual administrators of the Park on behalf of the Crown) for permission. Despite some local opposition this was granted and the first drives over this new course can be seen here.

4.

OPENING OF EXTENDED COURSE
STIRLING GOLF CLUB   JUNE 29.1912

The scene is Brisbane's sawmill in Wallace Street about 1910. In the background can be seen the level crossing keeper's cottage for the Forth & Clyde Junction Railway which crossed the main road here. A scene which has changed greatly especially over recent years. This is now the area covered by Tesco's car park at their filling station end.

THOMAS BRISBANE,
Wallace Street Sawmills,
===== STIRLING. =====

All kinds of Home Timber.
===== FIREWOOD. =====

The scenes shown here occurred in 1910 following the death of King Edward. 'The King is dead. Long live the King.' The new King, George the Fifth was proclaimed in Stirling on Wednesday 11 May 1910 at the traditional spots of the castle Esplanade, Market Cross and Burgh Gate. The local dignitaries who shared the honour of reading out the proclamation hailing the new monarch were Provost Bayne, Sheriff Lees and the Town Clerk D.B. Morris. After this last reading, the readers and their invited guests walked accompanied by their military escort to the door of the Golden Lion where the Councillors and invited guests disappeared inside to partake of some well earned refreshments after their gruelling day. Some aspects of everyday life do not change.

Although regattas had been held at other points on the river, it was not until 1854 that the first organized race took place at Stirling. There was another organized race the following year. In the meantime John MacFarlane, of Coneyhill, Bridge of Allan had given over a cheque for £200 to further boating and regattas at Stirling and a club was quickly formed. The busy scene in King Street which is shown here was photographed on Saturday 24 August 1894 and was organized by the boating club. The occasion was Stirling's first ever lifeboat Saturday and part of the procession through the town can be seen here. There were representatives from the Town Council, the Guildry, the Seven Incorporated Trades, the Castle, the Club itself and various

industries. As can be seen here there was also a lifeboat which was launched on the river at the regatta which was held upstream from the bridges. One feature of the regatta that day was a demonstration of buoyancy clothing made at the mills beside the Old Bridge. The guinea pig for this innovative clothing was Andrew Wilson, the science master at the High School. Note the shopfronts in the background and the variety of lamps. Crawford's the bookseller on the extreme left has its Royal Warrant above the door as well as its own outside light. The Temperance Hotel has only a door to the street but has a bit of advertising on its lamp. James Valentine (late George Nicolson) was to become Somerville and Valentine.

Stirling has had many benefactors throughout the ages and the names of a few appear in these pages. One of these was Thomas Stuart Smith whose legacy allowed for the building of the Smith Art Gallery and Museum, one of the town's under-rated assets. After an extensive search for a site in the town, the site in Dumbarton Road was chosen and the classical building that exists today was erected. Officially opened on Tuesday 11 August 1874 by Sir William Stirling-Maxwell of Keir. They were a bit wary about showing off the new Gallery's own collection initially and, indeed, borrowed resident's paintings to hang until they made sure that the atmosphere of the new building would not harm their treasures. One thing that local trustees and management had no scruples about was letting out the main gallery. All sorts of concerts and other public events were held here over a period of six years until Alfred Cox from Nottingham, one of the trustees, visited the town. He pointed out that this was illegal under the terms of the trust deed and should cease. A campaign was now organized; led by Dr Charles Allan, who was a noted locally based musician, to erect a new venue. The Stirling Public Hall Company Ltd was formed and the campaign came to a successful end with the erection of the Albert Halls. The new halls would not, in the eyes of its originators, be complete with an organ and a magnificent pipe organ costing £2,300 was purchased and once graced the back of the stage in the main hall. Part of this sum was raised from a 'Fancye Fayre', or giant sale of work, held in, of all places, the Smith. This 'Fayre' began on Thursday 24 August 1882 and ran for the next two days. The main Gallery became a mock medieval English village in which was a 'display and sale of feminine work never before seen in the Burgh'. The total realized was £2,730. Our photograph shows the stall-holders and their assistants posing before the bazaar was open to the public.

Today under its present able and progressive curator and her staff, the Smith Art Gallery and Museum houses many of the area's artistic and historical treasures and new exhibitions are regularly held. Many lectures and meetings are held in the lecture theatre and the shop and restaurant add to the ambience. The one abiding complaint is, however, rather mundane but nevertheless genuine. Is there a sponsor out there prepared to earn the eternal gratitude of hundreds of people by sponsoring new comfortable seats for the lecture theatre?

The Revd Dr Charles Rogers was responsible for changing the face of Stirling for ever. A chaplain at the Castle, he became a councillor, and had, among other attributes, a 'statue mania'. He was responsible for the acquisition of various statues including Wallace (at the top of King Street), Bruce (on the esplanade), the Martyr's Monument and the religious figures (in the Holy Rude churchyard) and above all was a major figure in the design, selection and fundraising for the National Wallace Monument. He was responsible for the removal of the old, decrepit wall round the Holy Rude churchyard and the laying out of the Mar's Garden and Valley sections of the same. He is commemorated in the area by a wrongly spelled street name in neighbouring Bridge of Allan, a poor reward for his work in the town and for his massive contribution to the recording of Scottish history and literature.

Sir John Murray came from Canada as a young man to live with his uncle, John MacFarlane at Coneyhill, Bridge of Allan. Always interested in science he was involved in experiments even then. One involved erecting an electric 'searchlight' in the days before electric light became a reality thus amazing and, indeed, terrifying many local residents. Another 'experiment' involving electricity was to lead to a dog belonging to a visitor (Sir John Hay, the Sheriff of Stirlingshire) and his uncle's dog getting an electric shock when they touched noses. This meant that each dog had thought the other had bitten it with the resulting mayhem that this brought to the MacFarlane household. John Murray became an internationally known figure by his work on bathymetrical surveys, firstly on the freshwater Lochs of Scotland, a project which started in partnership with Frederick Pattison Pullar. The partnership, however, ceased when the latter was drowned on 15 February 1901 in Airthrey Loch while attempting to save a Miss Kate Rutherford who had fallen through the ice covering the surface. He was, unfortunately unsuccessful and both perished. Sir John later went on to complete the Scottish survey and carried out many similar around the world.

> The Upper House of Parliament—they never work awa'
> They only gather in the House to pass their time awa'
> The silly cloited bodies, they hae neither sense nor skill
> Or they never would have rejected 'Gladstone's Franchise Bill

Although not taken in Stirling—indeed this early photograph was taken on the far side of
Wellsfield Farm on the Stirling to Dunipace Road—this procession was heading towards Stirling
to take part in a large political demonstration. The date is September of 1884 and here we see

> We working men of Carrongrove our banners here display,
> To root out the Tory Lords, we'll fight and win the day.

Four wagonloads of workers from Carrongrove Paper Mill took part. The white caps, which
they wear, all had the word Franchise printed on them. The gentleman on the horse heading
the contingent was William Lithgow whom one report describes as being dressed *a la* Robinson
Crusoe. He was actually dressed in fox's skins and a large cocked hat and was armed with a
sword and shield. Those responsible at the mill for part of the process involving straining water
from the paper carried on their banner 'We'll strain the House of Lords to the very dregs.' Over
5,000 workmen from all over the area gathered for the demonstration with contingents from as
far afield as Milngavie and Grangemouth. Meeting in the King's Park they paraded through the
town via Albert Place, Murray Place and Barnton Street. At Viewfield Place opposite the County
Buildings there was a bonfire lit. The marchers now proceeded via Queen Street while the carts
in the procession took the gentler route via Cowane Street, Union Street and Wallace Street
to join with the marchers back in Port Street. The marchers meantime had marched via Baker

Street and King Street. As many of the carts were fully loaded the easy route was a necessity. The shoemakers, for example, had set up a workshop on their cart complete with a banner stating 'Past mending like the House of Lords.'

Printers from the *Stirling Observer*—at that time the more radical of the local newspapers and not afraid to speak out against the injustices and incompetence and waste in central and local government—had a printing press on which they were printing and distributing a handbill containing verses. One of these read—

> Who set them up, those haughty peers
> The people to defy
> We'll bring their house about their ears
> And knock them into pie. [Pie is jumbled up printer's type]

The Fleshers had a white bullock escorted by two attendants who took turns riding on its back. All went well with this pair until, just before the speeches began back at the King's Park, their white and, until then, placid mount decided to create mayhem by taking off through the crowds.

After the two parts of the procession met up at the bottom of King Street, it proceeded via Port Street and Park Avenue to the King's Park. Everything, however, was not quite sunshine and light and at one point on the march there was an unfortunate incident, which was only prevented from becoming very serious for the perpetrators by the prompt action of the stewards. As the march passed along Albert Place, the daughters of the then late James Hogg of the *Stirling Journal*—a staunch Tory newspaper—and a male friend hung out a banner emblazoned 'Hurrah for the Lords' and started hurling abuse at the marchers who retaliated by storming the house before being restrained by the stewards.

Many interesting banners and relics appeared on the procession with many relating to the Radical Rising of 1820. One carter rode a horse with a pall for a saddle cloth. He was wearing the headsman's cloak and carrying the axe used at the execution in Stirling of John Baird and Andrew Hardie in 1820. This axe and cloak are now in the possession of the Smith Museum and Art Gallery. The axe was used in Glasgow the week before their execution to behead another Radical —James Wilson from Strathaven, who had the nickname Pearly or Purly as he was reputed to be the originator of the purl stitch. (Whisper it quietly but the axe was borrowed from Glasgow Town Council and never returned by that in Stirling. Moral—never lend Stirling Council any tools). The axe carried a large label stating 'Tory Logic 1820'. The present whereabouts of many of the other relics are unknown and the author (who has a particular and personal interest in the 1820 Rising) would dearly love to know where they are. For example, one of the Whins of Milton contingent carried a pole at the top of which was a cup from which his father had helped Baird and Hardie and the other Radicals to a drink as they were taken as prisoners to Stirling Castle after the Battle of Bonnymuir. The Bannockburn party wore tartan scarves and carried the banner carried at the Reform Act demonstrations of 1832. At least three of those present in 1884, ancestors of the author, had also been present in 1832. Two old men from Camelon carried a banner stating 'We are two veterans who carried bread and cheese to the Radicals at Bonnymuir 1820' while their names and ages were on the corners, 'Andrew Burt aged 74 years' and 'James Smith aged 81 years'. Two nailers from Camelon—James Burt and Andrew Burt Jnr—were arrested after Bonnymuir but it is not known at this time whether Andrew Jnr of 1820 and Andrew of 1884 were one and the same.

Although this is the only photograph to surface so far of this major political demonstration it is reported that Smart, a local photographer, who stayed in Viewfield Place had a camera set up on its tripod at his window to record the passing of the procession. Where are they?

Stirling County Cricket Club X1 who played the I Zingari touring X1 in a two-day game sponsored by Mrs Forbes of Herbertshire Castle at Dunipace (this was not long before the castle was destroyed by fire). I Zingari was one of the great groundless but touring only teams playing club, school and Service teams in the days before the First World War. The visitors won by an innings and 32 runs with Capt. R.H. Crake (of the K.O.S.B. regiment) excelling with a score of 102 before being caught by Ferguson. This gentleman was certainly not in the county team during this game as a batsman gaining 2 runs in the first innings and being run out for 1 in the second. There was a fair bit of inconsistent play from Stirling County in this game. A.M.P. Lyle was their highest scorer in their first innings with a credible 34 but only managing 1 run in the second. Maybe the orchestra and pipe band laid on as entertainment distracted him. Note how nice and fresh the pavilion behind is. It was at this stage only eleven years old having been bought second hand by the club following its initial spell of duty as a pavilion at the 1901 Glasgow Exhibition.

Henry Drummond was the grandson of William Drummond, the Stirling seedsman, who through his own deeds and those of his sons changed the face of Stirling. William had eleven sons. Henry (father of our Henry) took over the running of the seed company as its head. David ran the Dublin side of the business. Peter founded the Drummond Tract Enterprise. James and Andrew became successful clothing retailers and so it goes on. Young Henry was born at 1 Park Place on 17 August 1851. He was an eminent theologian and traveller writing on religion and on Africa as well as children's books. He was an early organizer in the Boy's Brigade movement and preached extensively. One of his books, *The Great Thing in the World* has never been out of print for over one hundred years, the latest edition coming from Samford University in Alabama, members of staff of which make regular pilgrimages to Stirling. Indeed, on 11 March 1997, the 100th anniversary of his death, the only people visiting his grave that day (wild wind and rain exactly as it was at his funeral) were Tom Corts, the President of Samford, and Marla, his wife. It appears that from available evidence Drummond's *Greatest Thing in the World* has sold over 10 million copies in nineteen languages. Professor Henry Drummond died at Tunbridge Wells on 11 August 1897 and was buried in the Holy Rude graveyard.

Tovey Tennent, who made the bulk of his assets working for the East India Company, helped change the face of the Top of the Town by getting Spittal's Yard cleared and the start made to the building of the High School of Stirling by making a substantial donation for this purpose. He is commemorated but one wouldn't know it. Go to Academy Road and walk along the frontage of what is now the Highland Hotel. About halfway between Spittal Street and the clock tower main entrance there can be seen a plain sandstone block surrounded a rope design set into the whin building stone. This was meant to be carved out with a message about this gentleman. In the 130-odd years of public ownership the local authorities never got round to it.

The Stirling Girl's Club came into existence in November 1901 and was intended as a place not really for pre teenage but for those in their teens and early twenties. Originally based at 18 The Bow, it soon moved to 28 Upper Bridge Street and finally into buildings in the grounds of Sauchie House in Baker Street which had been used as the laundry and bathrooms of the Boys Industrial School. They were open three or four nights a week and the young women were taught cooking, blouse making, and sewing while musical drill, singing, music and games formed their entertainment.

Many of the girls took advantage of a scheme whereby they were helped in dressmaking and paid weekly towards the cost of the clothes they were making. As a means of providing something for the young women to do it was an outstanding success although there was occasional disappointment expressed by the organizers that they had not been able to help some whose morals were not exactly one hundred per cent. Our photographs show part of the picnic for married members and children in June 1916 and an open-air concert at Beechwood in July 1919. Some of the children from Whinwell Home are seated at the front of the audience.

Whinwell Home for Destitute and Orphan Children

Founded 1884.

Supported by *Voluntary Contributions.*

Children are received from all parts of Scotland, and must be destitute.

Applications to be made to Miss CROALL, Secretary and Superintendent, Whinwell, Stirling.

Ex-Provost KINROSS.	J. JENKINS, Esq.
Ex-Provost THOMSON.	Miss HUNTER.
J. TEMPLETON, Esq.	Miss CROALL.

Physician—Dr. JAMES MURRAY, Abercromby Place.
Dentists—Messrs. BROWN & WILSON, Melville Terrace.
Solicitors—Messrs. A. & J. JENKINS, Port Street.
Banker—Mr. DANIEL FERGUSON, National Bank of Scotland.
Auditor—Mr. JAMES SMITH, Clydesdale Bank, King Street.

The interior of Allan Park Post Office in 1937. This sub-office has closed over recent years but was once a busy office serving a goodly part of the town. The counter display is quite interesting not just for the variety of items for sale but for the nice little pointer to a well-known aspect of the Royal Family's history. Note the Coronation jigsaw showing GeorgeV1 and Queen Elizabeth (the present Queen Mother) alongside souvenirs relating to his brother Edward. He was proclaimed King and the souvenir market was flooded with all kinds of geegaws. Edward abdicated, however, before he was crowned and many of the fancy goods manufacturers had to start all over again.

OUR NEW SUITINGS, TROUSERINGS, AND OVERCOATINGS are we worth seeing

THE TAILORING of same PERFECTION.

JAMES NICOL, TAILOR & CLOTHIER, 69, KING STREET, STIRLING.

During the early months of 1895 the whole of Scotland was held in the grip of a severe frost. One local effect here was that the River Forth was frozen over for a fortnight. For anyone who has not seen the River frozen over and can not visualize such a scene let it be said that another stretch of water frozen over that year was a major part of Loch Lomond. Our two photographs here show some of the residents on the ice at Cambuskenneth. Note how helpful the Town Council was by providing the planks seen in the lower picture. This was to make it easier for the *lieges* to get onto the ice. In this era of political correctness, of suing for the least thing, of counselling because one has missed the bus *et al* can anyone believe that any local authority, daft though many of them undoubtedly are, would do such a thing? Even if the 32 degrees of frost, which was what was recorded at one point, had frozen the Forth with three feet of ice.

Opposite top: Looking out on the Cornton Road towards the Causewayhead Road. Unfortunately the photographer has not really covered what we would like to see today. The extreme right-hand shows the edge of the Mill while the extreme left-hand side shows the edge of the Rubber Works and slight details of the house, which once stood there. On the opposite side of the road is part of the property of Raines, the thrashing contractor. The original founder of this company came to Scotland from Lincolnshire with the first portable thrashing machine to be seen in Scotland. This was the Clayton & Shuttleworth, which was pulled by horses, as was its portable steam engine. The firm lasted until 1946 when Shirlaw Allan, the auctioneers were called in to auction off the assets. One of the company's traction engines *Sir Hector* is now owned by the Scottish Agricultural Museum at Ingliston.

From the *Stirling Journal* of 20 February 1857:

Clayton & Shuttleworth's thrashing machine

> This apparatus has been engaged in this neighbourhood for the last eight or ten days and has attracted the attention and commanded the approbation of all our leading agriculturists. During the last two days, it has been engaged on the farms occupied by Mr Peter Dewar at Gartur and Gateside where, at the latter place, it may be seen in full operation today. The thrashing machine is constructed upon an entirely new principle. The machinery is contained in a wooden framework mounted on wheels for the purpose of its locomotion. The victual is put in at the top of this close framework, seized by the drum and carried into the body of the machine. Nothing more is seen of it till the straw appears thrown out by the shakers at one end, the chaff at the other end and the corn is dropped into bags at the side. The machine is driven by a small portable engine of about eight horsepower and is capable of thrashing upwards of ten bolls of oats per hour. On Wednesday last 84 bolls were thrashed at Gartur within eight hours. We understand that the proprietor of the machine is to be engaged for some time yet in the district. The charge for the use of the apparatus for one day is £2.2/-

Opposite bottom: Our other photograph shows one of Raines' 'big mills' in operation on a local farm, possibly King's Park Farm, about the beginning of the 1920s.

The 1911 Coronation of King George V was celebrated in style in Stirling and these photographs show part of the procession organized through the town. Our photographer, in this case Mark Bennet, is positioned in the Bank of Scotland building at the bottom of King Street. Originally built as offices and warehouses for the Drummond Tract Enterprise, this building was once adorned with profiles of Scottish Reformers and with a marble group of angels above the corner. The Tract Enterprise vacated this building to relocate to Dumbarton Road where the building was built for them there is now partly occupied by Scottish Power. In its heyday the Tract Enterprise was sending up to half a ton of mainly single page tracts per day. The volume of business generated by them was such that Stirling Post Office had to keep moving to larger premises culminating in the opening of the present Post Office building in 1865.

A busy playtime scene at one of the Stirling primary schools. Ah, but where? Erected following the 1872 Education Act this primary served the lower part of the town. Situated next to Brighton Place (still there), its frontage faced George Street (now gone completely), it is the Craigs Primary School, the site of which is now occupied by the multi-storey National Car Park. Many former pupils of the Craigs school still look with affection on their time there and all Stirling residents should look with affection on the car park. After all they are paying for it in more senses than the obvious one of paying their parking charge. How many realize that it was built under the encouragement of the now defunct Central Regional Council where officials in their 'wisdom' agreed that a subsidy should be paid annually to NCP for the first twenty years of operation. Oh that such payments came from the personal salaries of such officials! The one good thing that officials did ensure was that the building could be converted to office space if it became redundant as a car park. Indeed, the top floors are on the books of a local commercial estate agent at this moment.

The local Oddfellows en route to Stirling station. They are coming along Murray Place just at the corner of Station road. The old Thistle Street and Orchard Place are in the background. Many of these branches raised money for outside charitable and other events. When the flagpole at the Borestone was erected in 1870 it was paid for by Oddfellows. A plaque was recently returned to grace the bottom of the flagpole after languishing for many years in the basement of the National Trust centre. It credits Loyal Dixon Lodge No.70 of Dumbarton with the erection. In actual fact they paid for the pole while the Stirling Lodge paid for the site work, guy ropes and foundations.

On July 1914 King George V and his wife, Queen Mary visited Stirling. They were welcomed to the town at the then County Buildings, now the Sheriff Court. One important function that he performed while there was to lay the foundation stone of the Municipal Buildings in the Corn Exchange. There was at that time a lot of disquiet over the Council's decision to build such a magnificent edifice while the Top of the Town, where the majority of the town's poorer residents lived, was one giant slum. The arrangement arrived at was that, at one stage in the proceedings, the King pressed a button and, via a cable strung through the streets and closes between Viewfield and Corn Exchange, an electric current was used to ring a bell and an unknown mason laid the foundation stone. On the left hand side of the central entrance is a carved stone stating foundation stone laid by King George V. The actual foundation stone laid that day is that immediately below. The two photographs on this page cover this stage of the proceedings and show a section of the invited guests and the tour round the Castle

A competition of unknown date but of obvious popularity taking place at the Stirling Bowling Club's green in Dumbarton Road. This club started life in 1854 playing alongside the Guildhall Bowling Club on the green beside Cowane's Hospital. This, incidentally, is the oldest green in continuous use in the country dating back to the beginning of the eighteenth century. In 1858, the club obtained agreement from the patrons of Spittal's Hospital for the feu of an area of ground on Dumbarton road east of the Double Hedges (the Back Walk from Academy Road to Dumbarton Road). It contracted Alexander MacDonald, who had a market garden in Barnton Street, to lay out the green. The opening match was played on 3 July 1858 although it was not until July 1866 that the club could open their very distinctive club house and replace their temporary pavilion.

This smart turnout was for the 1902 Coronation Parade. The young ladies represented the firm of Wylie & Sanderman, who had their steam laundry premises at the bottom of Abbey Road. If one can take one's eyes away from the pretty dresses and pretty (though, for the camera, not very happy) faces one can see in the background the jetty for the Cambuskenneth ferry and the houses at the river's edge of the village. One point to note is the company name in small letters on the offside of the cart. Legal requirements of the time (and still applicable to lorries) meant that the owner had to have his name on the nearside of any cart used on the public roads. There are, however, various entries in the local papers of owners, mostly farmers, being fined in court for this offence.

This happy band of young Stirling residents was photographed in November of 1912 in the Craigs. They are ready for the opening of the Electric Theatre, the first regular cinema in the town. It had been converted from a garage and during the 1980s reverted to this use becoming the depot for Autoglass. Moving pictures actually appear to have come from the Stirling area at, of all places, Deanston. The *Stirling Journal* notes that a cinematograph show will be given as part of the opening ceremony for the primary school there. No details are known at this stage about this show. We then find references to moving pictures being given as part of concert shows. The two main organizers of such events were Coutts' Renowned Scotch Troubadours Company and the Calder Cinematograph Company. The latter certainly had their own camera operators who filmed special events in the area visited and showed them locally. When nothing special was happening they filmed local school children thus guaranteeing them an audience. Elsewhere in this book there can be seen an Oddfellows procession heading for the Stirling station in order to embark on a day trip to Aberdeen. Calder, the following week, showed the Oddfellows enjoying themselves in the Granite City. After the Electric Theatre opened there was, in the following years, other cinemas in the town. The Kinema in December 1915; the Picture House in February 1921; the Queens in 1928; the Regal in October 1932 and the Allanpark in October of 1938. Films were also shown in the Alhambra, which was the music hall in the Arcade; in the Olympia (which had initially been built to satisfy demand when a huge roller skating craze swept Britain at the end of the first decade of the twentieth century); the Randolph (which was owned and operated by the Miner's Welfare). Apart from the Allanpark, all of these have ceased their original function or have been demolished totally. Only the Alhambra, part of a retail unit in the Arcade, and the Electric, now retail, in the Craigs actually remain. All the 'big name' films were shown in Stirling although, at times, audience reaction has not always been what the owners expected. A good example of this occurred in 1947 when part of the programme included a short film called *Birth of a Baby*. Many people in the audience (mostly men) fainted and ambulances had to be in attendance at every performance. What is it that women say? 'If men had babies the world's population would drop dramatically'

At the end of the First World War the government declared that 19 August 1919 should be declared 'Joy Day'. Stirling, however, waited until the Monday, 1 September, in order to hold their Victory Day. The day was declared a public holiday and a full range of events organized. There was only a limited show of public illuminations at the head of King Street and there was no fireworks display. The Council decided that, because of the cost, this would not be held. A far cry from today when, at the least excuse, local council officials spend money as though it was going out of fashion to put on a temporary display and even going as far as trying to burn a sculpture of one of Scotland's national heroes, Robert the Bruce, as part of a firework display to mark the current millennium mania. The council in 1919, however, did ask the residents to light up as many windows as possible to create the illusion. A large, mainly military, parade was held through a major part of the town. Shown here is the town's Victory car with Miss M. Buchanan of Broad Street in the place of honour representing Britannia, surrounded by various local girls representing America, France, Belgium and Italy. The Victory car has reached the Corn Exchange where a saluting stand outside the Municipal Buildings held the Duke of Montrose and General F.C. Davies, GOC Scottish Command. Other events that day included a children's procession, sports events and open air dancing.

The date is 1936 and here we have the photographers being caught on camera. Jimmy Nairn and his team are busily filming part of the restoration of the Holy Rude Church. He was the manager of the Regal Cinema and was heavily involved in the life of the town. One of those causes, which he supported wholeheartedly, was the fundraising for Stirling Royal Infirmary. He organized after-film show concerts in the cinema and helped with charity football matches . Part of one of those concerts is shown in the other photograph starring another indefatigable charity worker, Wee Jackie McCall, who always seemed cheery and was always at the forefront in charity events making fun of himself. A sadly missed character in the area! Our other photograph shows one such concert party act on the stage of the Regal with wee Jackie on the right.

During the restoration one major task was the removal of a wall erected in 1656 to divide the Holy Rude into the East and West Churches. This came about due to controversy between the Revd James Guthrie and his assistant, Mathias Symson. The Town Council was responsible for the appointment of ministers, a point that Guthrie did not approve of. The compromise of a physical division of the building did not prevent Guthrie from fighting against local and central authority and he was eventually executed in Edinburgh in 1661 and his head erected on a spike at the Netherbow in Edinburgh. Guthrie's head was removed in 1688 by Alexander Hamilton who himself became minister of the Holy Rude in 1726. Guthrie's last sermon, on religious freedom, was the first preached by a later minister there, Ebenezer Erskine, when he was removed from his charge for preaching on the same subject and had to hold his first services in the graveyard.

Although there was an earlier attempt at running a co-operative in Stirling, it was not until August 1880 that Stirling Co-operative Society was formed. Its predecessor actually failed about 1840 and the then manager, John Yuil, emigrated to Australia where he is represented today by his many descendants. Stirling was a bit slower off the mark than the neighbouring village of Bannockburn, whose Co-operative Society, with the active encouragement of the mill-owning Wilson family, was founded in 1834. Although starting from fairly modest beginnings the Stirling Society, by careful management, flourished and had various branches and shops all over the town. The event is unknown but is possibly the 1911 Coronation procession.

One traditional task that the Town Council used to undertake was the safeguarding of the towns' ancient boundaries by walking round them every year. Four parties of councillors would each head for a different area and the extent of the boundaries would be marked. The group standing in line are the important ones in the ceremony. They are the birleymen and it was their responsibility to dig out a sod of earth at each designated spot. This tradition has been ignored for the last fifty years and the now defunct *Stirling Journal* newspaper in an article from the time could explain why. It had only just been revived after being in abeyance after going from a yearly event to a seven-yearly event. The newspaper's editor thought councillors would discover themselves in streets they didn't know existed or in streets they wished did not exist The same applies today but, as well as councillors, the group should include officials, many of whom live outwith the district and do not know the areas on which they are making far reaching decisions.

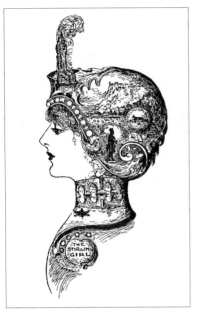

Above left: See how many famous Stirling features you can see in this twenties flapper girl. Drawn by John G. Mathieson, a local art dealer and framer, it is an ingenious guide to the town. The son of the artist is better known to a world-wide audience. He was Muir Mathieson, who either composed or conducted (or both) the music for dozens of British films in the middle of this century.

Above right: During The First World War many civilians were involved on the Home Front with, for example, many women taking over traditional men's work and many others taking part in voluntary work. This photograph show one aspect of such voluntary work, which was fundraising. Other tasks taken on by women and girls in this area was the collecting and preparation of spaghnum moss for the use in the dressing of wounds. This photograph, taken outside the Golden Lion Hotel in King Street, has obviously been part of a successful day on behalf of the war-injured horses.

Opposite bottom: Over one hundred years ago a petition to construct a bridge to give access to Cambuskenneth was launched and an anonymous donor even offered to loan the sum required but there was disagreement between the County Council and the Town Council and the scheme fell through. By the beginning of the 1930s there were renewed calls for a bridge and even calls to evacuate the community from their isolation in the manner of the population evacuation of St Kilda. Those wanting a bridge had their way and, by 1935, a new bridge was designed and constructed by Christiani & Neilson of London. Our photograph shows the old ferry and construction work underway on the new bridge which opened officially on 23 October 1935.

Stirling Scouts parade in the King's Park. Originally founded by Baden-Powell, the Boy Scout Movement was quickly established in the Stirling area. A group of Scouts led by Sergeant Penny, a Bannockburn ex-soldier, caught the attention of Major Frederick Maurice Crum. He was also a military gentleman and had served in India and in the Boer War where he was one of the first to meet Winston Churchill after the latter escaped from the Boers. He was later to be in charge of training snipers during the First World War. Major Crum devoted the rest of his life to helping young boys through the Scout Movement and through the foundation of the Boy's Club at the Top of the Town. He stated that his first sighting of Scouts was when he met Sergeant Penny's troop. During the conversation a car went past and the Sergeant promptly saluted. When asked who was in the car, the Sergeant replied 'I do not know but if he has a car, he must be an officer'! Remember, this was 1909 but, even then, Major Crum was amazed at the reply.

One factor in the decline of Stirling as a port, albeit of fairly limited access, was the arrival of the railway system. Many of the early meetings of the River Commissioners discuss the arrival of the Scottish Central Railway in 1848 and how the railway lines would cut off ready access to the shore. They did, however, continue trying to remove the various shoals and fords downstream. Stirling did manage to survive for a number of decades and the port was involved, for example, in shipping out prefabricated buildings, manufactured in the town, for use in Australia during that country's gold rush in the 1850s. There also was, for a time in the latter part of the last century, a small but thriving ship building yard turning out ships of up to three hundred tons.

A crushing blow, again railway-inspired, came in the late 1870s when a new railway bridge at Throsk was built. Although this was a swing bridge it was constructed on one of the bends in the river and precedence was given to trains. Some of the passenger steamships overcame the difficulties of the bridge being closed by having fold-down masts and funnels. Most traffic ceased although passenger steamers did run until the First World War and one of the deciding factors in the Ordnance Depot being established in the 1880s was river access and the fact that the Wilson's in Cambuskenneth were contractors (with coastal steamers) to the War Department. Although constructed down river from the town this bridge did have a major effect on Stirling and is worthy of inclusion here. This photograph shows the result of one of the many accidents involving shipping. This one took place in 1906. The piers are all that remain now but, of course, it is now too late for any substantial traffic to return to one of Europe's most underused major rivers.

The town has, at the present moment, an ideal opportunity to revitalize the upper stretch of the river at the town. The redevelopment of the Forthside area should provide leisure space and the facilities to turn the most underused river of its size in Western Europe into an exciting water-based complex. Instead the thoughts of the local authorities revolve around the creation of more shopping space for national and international retail companies, a policy which will spell the final death knell of the small retail businesses which are, at present, hanging on by their fingertips in the traditional shopping areas of the town.

Wilson first contract and read to the Meeting
the following report from Mess.rs Stevenson
"Edinburgh June 13th 1859 Forth Navigation Dear Sir
"Having in terms of your letter of 31st ulto. reported
"inspected the Forth Navigation, and met with a
"Committee of the Commissioners we have to recom-
mend that the works be taken off the hands of Mr.
Wilson the Contractor and that the percentages
which have been retained be paid to him less
any sum that may be found deficient in the
valuation of the plant belonging to the Com-
-missioners which in terms of the agreement

Although Stirling was for many hundreds of years a seaport the river trade was slowing down by the turn of the turn of the twentieth century and more or less ceased a few years later on the outbreak of the First World War, never really recovering after hostilities ceased.

During the nineteenth century Stirling saw the direct importation of tea from China and of timber from the Baltic. The Forth, however, has always been restricted because of the number of bends—the Links o' Forth—and by shoals and in certain sections by its unusual tidal flow—the Leckies—where the tide moves in opposite directions at different depths. The only surviving minute book of the Commissioners of the River Forth shows details of some of the attempts to clear these shoals. This passage details, as engineer in charge, a certain Mr Stevenson. This was the father of the future author, Robert Louis Stevenson, and, on this occasion, he brought his wife and young Robert to stay at nearby Bridge of Allan. The *Stirling Journal* for this week reports Mr and Mrs Stevenson and Mr Louis Stevenson being visitors to the spa town. With the opening of the Alloa Swing Bridge at the Throsk in the late 1870s the river traffic was cut dramatically. Trains had precedence over ships at this swing bridge and some of the passenger steamship companies used ingenious methods to negotiate the hazard. The Galloway Steam Packet Company's vessels had, for example, folding masts and funnels which the crew brought down onto the deck to allow the ship to duck under the bridge.

At the outbreak of the First World War the Admiralty closed all the small ports on the river and after hostilities the only new traffic was, for a number of years, a weekly delivery of ninety tons to the Anglo American Oil Company's depot. In November 1931 the MV *Nollijia* brought in a load of 170 tons of special sand for the use of the town's waterworks from Bridport in Dorset. In 1933 the MacEwan (Stirling) Grain Company took delivery of 250 tons of potash from Antwerp and both this company and James Gray & Co were to bring in reasonable quantities of fertilizer annually. This ceased again with the outbreak of the Second World War. Ships again came up after the end of hostilities but only one or two and eventually trade ceased altogether. Facilities fell into disrepair and there is now next to nothing to show that Stirling was once a port.

Another Royal Visit to the town by Queen Mary, this time in 1938 after her husband King George V had died. The Royal car is shown here at the top of St John Street. An enthusiastic crowd of mainly women do their best to glimpse the old queen although one young lady just to left of centre foreground seems more intent on presenting herself to our photographer who, in this case, was John G. 'Squire' Wilson of Bannockburn.

A fine view of the *Stirling Observer* office in the Craigs during the First World War. Note the vast number of recruiting posters of all types. Like many local papers the *Observer* published a list of dead and wounded locals. This was a practice which was soon abandoned as the lists became horrendously long. The columns of the local papers show dozens of local lads and not so local lads of Stirling extraction fighting in every imaginable unit and listed as dead, missing in action, wounded or prisoners. Perhaps the fine military gentleman on the left became one of them. I do not know.

Three

The Military

A busy scene in King Street in 1934. As part of a recruiting drive the Scots Greys ride round Scotland trying to get new recruits prepared to ride their grey mounts into battle against such incidentals as the modern tanks with which Germany was re-arming. An idea that was soon to be abandoned. The regiment whose horses are now kept for ceremonial occasions redid the journey for the sixtieth anniversary and the dozen or so troopers riding across Stirling's Old Bridge and through the town were certainly an impressive sight. No wonder the crowds were out in force in 1934 to see the major part of the regiment ride through.

In 1908 the part-time soldiers of Britain were reorganized and the old Volunteers became the Territorials. The first summer camp of the local Argyll Territorials was held on the edge of the town at Birkhill on the Cambusbarron Road. Over three thousand members of the local regiments' territorial battalions attended; part of their camp can be seen here in this Mark Bennet photograph.

The 7th Batallion of the Argyll and Sutherland Highlanders was the local territorial battalion of the world famous regiment. They went to war in 1914 but before they went it was not all training for combat. They had lighter moments and this one shows the football team organized by B Company. Unbeaten wherever they played, they had a secret weapon. No, not the grim looking officers or the even grimmer looking sergeants used to frighten the opposition. They had an extra man! There are twelve of the 'Ladies from Hell'.

Not all of Stirling's part-time soldiers, whether Volunteers or later Territorials, were members of the Argyll and Sutherland Highlanders. Some of the big boys wanted to play with big toys. Here is the local company of the Royal Garrison Artillery with one of their toys.

Members of our local company of the Royal Garrison Artillery posing with their mascot outside the Roxburgh Arms in North Queensferry while at summer camp in 1903.

Stirling Castle, July 1917. The gentleman with his back to us is Samuel McDonald and the military gentleman facing him and to our right is Colonel Sir P. Potter who is taking part in this little ceremony in his role of commanding officer of Stirling Castle. In his last public engagement before moving on he is presenting a Distinguished Conduct Medal which had been gained by Mr McDonald's son. Unfortunately for young Samuel McDonald the honour had been gained posthumously. On 15 September 1916 members of the Canadian Expeditionary Force were at the forefront of an attack on the German lines. The leading company was in charge of two corporals, both of whom were lost almost immediately. Private McDonald took charge and continued in command almost all day. At one stage in the engagement only two other bombers and himself were left to fight off a counterattack by almost thirty Germans. Despite these overwhelming odds the three soldiers coolly threw down their grenades and broke up the counter attack. Unfortunately for our hero he was so severely wounded that he died soon afterwards. He is buried in a military cemetery near Poziers. Although with the Canadians, young Samuel and his two brothers, Ronald and John (who was also killed in the war) were local lads who had emigrated from Bridge of Allan to Canada a number of years before the war.

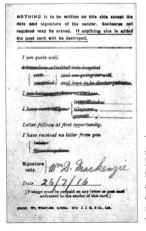

This standard postcard was sent to Stirling in 1916 by D. Mackenzie after injury at the front. The impersonal 'delete as appropriate' format was designed to prevent sensitive information falling into the wrong hands.

When the First World War broke out in August 1914 there were large numbers of people willing to fight. (After all everyone was told the war would only last until Christmas.) These men had to be trained and equipped and, as Stirling had been an ordnance depot since the 1880s, it was natural that this area became a giant training ground. Within a few months over 11,000 men were here, halls and buildings of all descriptions were requisitioned and life here changed dramatically. Apart from requisitioned buildings such as Hayford Mill, the Smith, Museum Hall at Bridge of Allan and the Albert Halls temporary accommodation was erected. This included huts on the Esplanade (later occupied by a Canadian lumberjack Battalion cutting down timber everywhere for the war effort) and a large camp at the Cornton. Comforts for the troops were provided by individuals and by various organizations. Our photograph here shows a large group of soldiers posing within the hut at Cornton provided by the Young Men's Christian Association. In this hut they could chat, have a cuppa, write letters home and generally get away from army life for a little while without being exposed to the 'fleshpots of iniquity' such as Bridge of Allan and Causewayhead. As many young fellows of these settlements have thought over the years, 'Chance would be a fine thing'.

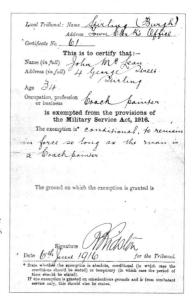

Local Tribunal: Name *Stirling (Burgh)*
Address *Town Clerk's Office*
Certificate No. *61*

This is to certify that:—

Name (in full) *John McLean*
Address (in full) *4 George Street*
Stirling
Age *34*
Occupation, profession or business *Coach painter*
is exempted from the provisions of the **Military Service Act, 1916.**

The exemption is* *conditional, to remain in force so long as the man is a Coach painter*

The ground on which the exemption is granted is

Signature *RKDalton*
Date *6th June 1916*   for the Tribunal.

* State whether the exemption is absolute, conditional (in which case the conditions should be stated) or temporary (in which case the period of time should be stated).

If the exemption is granted on conscientious grounds and is from combatant service only, this should also be stated.

The scene is the quadrangle of the High School of Stirling building in Spittal Street (now the Highland Hotel). The date is July 1918 and the school cadets are on parade. During the First World War, a strong cadet force with progression to the forces was not the only contribution made by the school. Domestic and technical teaching was geared to military essentials. Instead of the knife box that I laboriously constructed or the model ship (instantly launched as the SS *Firewood*) that one of my sons made, the technical department turned out wooden trench periscopes on a production line basis. For the school's efforts it was presented with a trophy of war—a real live working German machine gun! The town for its efforts received a tank which, until it was sold to Ben McKenzie for scrap just before the Second World War, stood on the grass at the top of Broad Street.

Four

Transport

Although many of the photographs in this book show scenes that have changed and events that no longer happen some things do not change. This photograph shows one such event that demonstrates this. Here we have a nice 'freebie' for councillors, officials and their good ladies. On Friday 11 July 1919 the Falkirk and District Tramway Company took the assembly shown above on a trip to Lochearnhead and back round via Crieff and Gleneagles. This was meant to celebrate the inauguration of a new bus service in the Stirling area and was in direct competition to the tramway company and the smaller local operators. None of the company appear to be in the least bit worried that many of these were going to disappear from business. At least the company paid for the outing and the food and drink consumed were not paid for by the Stirling peoples' rates and taxes as so often happens.

Although some journeys were within the precincts of the town, buses were of great advantage to those people who had to travel into or out of town. Here is a fine example of early bus transport., taken outside Langarth opposite Snowdon Place. The three horses are not for speed but for pulling power. This photograph was taken by Robert F.W. Blakey in 1908 when he was only about fourteen and I am indebted to his descendants in Canada for giving me a copy of it.

This photograph was not taken in Stirling but it shows the Belhaven, of Taylor of Bannockburn, MS 74 ready to leave from outside Bannockburn New Town Hall on its journey into town. Robert Taylor had been operating horse buses from at least, 1894 and actually owned the first vehicle in Stirlingshire to be registered as a public conveyance. After his death, Robert Taylor's business was run by his son (also Robert) until his untimely death at the age of thirty-two in June 1920. The business was sold to Scottish General Omnibus Company on 6 May 1921.

Although primarily a bus picture there are many points of interest here in this photograph of AMS 582. On the right the driver of another single decker can be seen retrieving something from the boot (two swing doors) of his vehicle. An open step, double-decker is just coming out of the bus station but behind it can be seen part of the gas works while on the left of AMS 582 can be seen the shop part of Stewart's Thistle Café. The sit-down meal section was missed by our photographer. This busy little shop was demolished to make way for the Thistle Centre. No, I do not think the shopping centre was named after Stewart's but when one realizes how little imagination emanates from local authorities perhaps it did. The gas works, owned by Stirling Gas Lighting Company Ltd, had occupied this site since 1826 with the first street lamps being lit on 27 November of that year. In 1845, 1874 and 1896 there were calls for the Town Council to take over the company but they never did.

Generally William Murdoch is given credit for the invention of gas lighting but he actually got the idea after hearing a conversation at the Boulton & Watt foundry in Birmingham between the owners and Archibald Cochrane, the 9th Earl of Dundonald, who lived at Culross just down river from Stirling. The Earl in his quest to produce tar for ship's hulls had been troubled by gas coming from the coal. He had flared this off using an old musket barrel. He then promptly ignored what was a more significant discovery but did mention it when in Birmingham. What would he have thought today if, looking across the river from Culross to Grangemouth, he could see the vast amount of gas being flared off at the refinery complex?

In these days of bus deregulation, one is becoming accustomed to seeing buses from different companies in town and buses going to more exotic destinations. (Are Southampton and Bristol and such like places really exotic?) Stirling had its own distinctive form of local transport, The Stirling & Bridge of Allan Tramway Company. This august body opened for business on 27 July 1874 and ceased operation on 5 February 1920. An advertisement in the *Stirling Observer* for 4 January 1872 states that 'Tramway Carriages are large and luxuriously fitted up' but take a look at this photograph of car 19. Luxury? Bah! Humbug! Look also at the horses which when the service finished were unfit for sale and went to the knacker's yard. One story goes thus: Glasgow resident—In Glasgow we have acetylene lamps on our trams.' Stirling resident—'Well, we can do better than that. We have a set of lean horses on our trams.'

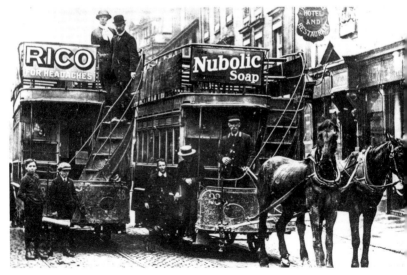

This photograph shows car 23 with a full complement of passengers passing the Sheriff Court. On occasion passengers actually had to get off at the Rob Roy public house to allow the horses an easier pull up the little snib just before the level ground shown here.

Opposite bottom: As built initially, the line ran from Henderson Street in Bridge of Allan to Port Street. Although most car journeys terminated at a double line loop at the bottom of King Street. Here are cars 48 and 23 with the Waverley Hotel and the Olympia Steps in the background. This is now the central entrance to the Thistle Centre. Again look at the rundown condition of the cars and the horses although, admittedly, this photograph was taken in the final years of the system.

On 29 January 1898 a new service was opened from King Street to St Ninians. This was first mooted twenty-five years before but had never been implemented. A trace horse was now necessary to help pull the cars up the incline to Woodlands. This trace horse was generally kept in command of a young boy just beyond the Wellgreen lane. In July 1878 the company experimented with a steam car. This innovation underwent two night-time trials before being run along a trial journey during the busiest time of the day. Special permission was granted to allow it to be used for the Bridge of Allan Games in the first week of August. This was a highly successful outing for the steam car with people clamouring to get aboard. Due to various objections, however, this was its only outing and it was laid up never to be used again.

In 1913, however, motorized bus transport was starting to provide serious competition for the horse-drawn trams and the company had one of the cars rebuilt as a petrol-driven vehicle. This is seen here posed at Bridge of Allan. Various attempts to electrify and extend the system were made at the beginning of the century but they all fell through. The most ambitious of these envisaged trams running from Dollar, Alloa, Dunblane and Denny while one extension would link with the Falkirk Tramway system at Larbert giving access to Lauriston and Grangemouth. All that was built of this ambitious layout was a spur from the Falkirk circular system to Lauriston. Local residents can, however, see one beneficial result of this abortive extension programme. Borestone Crescent at St Ninians was constructed to save the trams having to negotiate the St Ninians old town. The line never extended beyond the Caledonian Buildings at St Ninians and, although the company tried to enter the bus field with the purchase of two Tilling-Stevens buses in November 1919, by May of 1920 journeys ceased with the sale of the company to the Scottish General Omnibus Company.

An empty Stirling harbour, c.1900.

Picture postcards were often produced very rapidly to keep up with major events. This 1914 postcard was issued to commemorate the visit of King George and Queen Mary to Stirling and was on sale less than a week after the event. It shows the royal Daimler outside the Municipal Buildings. The message on the back is as interesting as the picture itself.

POST

Communication

Stirling 16-7-14.

Dear Aggie. Had a great time with Ryally last Saturday. This Picture shows them Just arrived. The King is shaking hands with the Provost's daughter. the Provost is shaking hands with the Queen. It is not generally known that the King is so bald. he has only a Patch on his Brow. this picture of his back view shows how bare his head is of hair. Are you coming Cally. thro' Edinburgh it is easiest to get from Edinigh to Stg by Cally. Trains leave Princes St Stn at 9-25 11-30. 1. 1-25. - leave Waverley Stn. per NBR. at 9-6. 12-58. let me know if you can, which way you are likely to come.

From the beginning of the century when the bicycle was king of personal transport this view was taken at the Drip Bridge and shows Cuthill's bicycle shop and a fine array of bikes. From the Drip Bridge out the Blairdrummond Road was a popular course for the racers of the day and Cuthill's shop (he also hired out some of the boats seen in so many early photos or postcards of the Old Bridge) was a favourite gathering point.

D. & J. MacEwen and Co. was founded in 1804 and was to become the town's premier and longest-lived grocery concern with branches locally and at Callander, Killin, Oban, Inverness, etc. Even last century they were at the forefront of the mercantile life of the town with, for example, direct imports of tea from China from 1835. This is their first delivery van photographed on a fine day. It would not be very pleasant in the cab when it was raining or snowing.

Unfortunately, MacEwen's at the corner of Port Street and Dumbarton Road (now part of their premises are occupied by Nationwide Building Society while the rest has been demolished) has gone and the passer-by now no longer has the opportunity to get a caffeine intake from the smell of freshly ground coffee which is a joy that has now gone. Next time you stand waiting at the supermarket checkout while cards, coupons, etc., are sorted out think of how pleasant and time saving it was having a real 'old-fashioned' grocer serve you and how much money was saved because of a control over impulse buying.

The town of Stirling was linked to the Scottish Central Railway in 1848 and this changed the face of Stirling completely. It was a contributory factor in the decline of river traffic. It allowed visitors to the town a much quicker and easier mode of transport thus increasing the tourist trade. It allowed commuting between the town and the major cities of Glasgow and Edinburgh and it allowed easier access for commerce and industry in the town to major and expanding markets. Even with the advent of lines by the Stirling & Dunfermline Railway and the Forth & Clyde Junction Railway, Stirling station remained fairly primitive. Even the railway amalgamations of the 1860s did little to improve matters. It was not until 1916 that the

station as we know it today was constructed. This view of platform 3 was taken shortly after this date. Note the prominence of Menzies bookstalls (after all, Stirling was one of the first railway bookstalls opened by this company) and of Malcolm Campbell's fruit stall. The girls beside the stall both have trays. They are the mobile buffet for passengers and are ready to move forward to sell their wares to people on the tray. Impossible to do now! Why? There are no windows which open nowadays to allow a transaction such as this to take place. Gone are the days of sliding windows whose up and down progress could be arrested by a thick leather strap with holes punched at intervals ready to affix to the large brass peg.

Stirling Railway Station, North Platform.

2193

This view of platform 2 was taken at around the same date.

Elder the Baker's new Ford van. Licensed on 18 October 1915, it was chocolate and gold in colour. Unfortunately, it did not stay pristine forever and was broken up on 18 October 1932.

This fire engine of 'the most modern improvement' was purchased by the Town Council in 1869 at a cost of £140 and was to see service until the beginning of the century. Although horse-drawn the engine was accompanied on its way by some of the firemen pushing wheelbarrows with extra hoses and all the other accessories required.

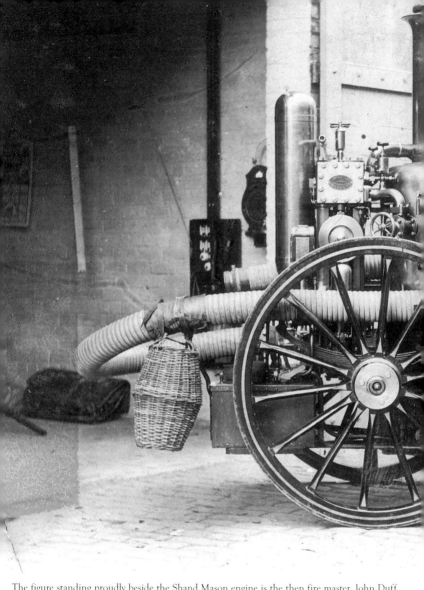

The figure standing proudly beside the Shand Mason engine is the then fire master, John Duff, an advert for whose services as a plumber is seen overleaf.

Above and overleaf: These fine photographs show the town's new Shand Mason fire engine being tested in 1905 before its acceptance by the Council. The new engine was supplied to the town at a cost of £265 including training of the brigade members and various warranty conditions. The new engine was shown off to a public who, in general, had been sceptical of the town's part-time brigade being able to contain any reasonably sized fire. The gentleman in the bowler hat walking beside the engine is the representative of the manufacturers. Height tests were made—note the hose snaking up over the town wall—and also suction tests out of the river. Everything was satisfactory and the new engine accepted. From our point of view today, however, a photograph of the most spectacular height test, has not, as yet, turned up. This test was carried out in King Street at the Steeple where the brigade with their new toy scooted water into the air to see if they could reach higher than the building. The other photograph is of the old engine, which was bought in 1869 at a cost of £140.

FIRE, SNOWDEN PLACE STIRLING, SEPT 23RD

Devastation by fire. On 23 September 1910 the owner of this house in Snowdon Place (almost at the corner with Melville Terrace) heard rustling behind the timber panelling. She suspected fire and telephoned down to John Duff, who had had a long association with the brigade and can be seen proudly standing beside the Shand Mason fire engine on the cover photograph. As well as being the owner of the major plumbing company in the town, he was agent for Minimax fire extinguishers. He called out the brigade and then jumped on his bike with a Minimax under his arm and cycled up to Snowdon Place. His efforts, the efforts of the brigade who arrived shortly afterwards and the efforts of the castle engine and soldiers, who had also been called out, were in vain. As can be seen the house was completely gutted although passing it today one would not suspect that anything untoward had ever happened there.

In August of 1923, the Town Council decided to buy a motor-powered fire engine instead of the horse-drawn Shand Mason steam-powered engine and its attendant wheelbarrows. They had, by this time, added a hired motor car to the fire service by taking advantage of an offer by George Owen, one of the car dealers in town, who agreed to keep a car available at all times for £5 per year. This photograph shows the result. One Dennis fire engine fitted with pneumatic tyres and hauling a trailer pump. Two covers for the radiators of both; two electric heaters for under the radiators in winter; two waterproof covers for the men; two extra lamps; two firemen's accumulator lamps and various structural alterations to the engine and its tender. All this for the princely sum of £471 10s 0d. Just before this new engine was tested (at the harbour in Riverside) and accepted, the inadequacies of the old horse-drawn steamer were amply demonstrated when a disastrous fire occurred at Auchentroig House at Buchlyvie. On the way there the brigade was met by the owner on his way to Stirling looking for them. Horses were uncoupled and the steamer hauled to Buchlyvie behind the owner's car!

No, the cans carried by some of the firemen in this photograph have nothing to do with a delay in wages and the two or three fancy dress characters have nothing to do with frightening youngsters away from fires. The brigade are taking part in a charity event—possibly Stirling Royal Infirmary week when funds were collected for the upkeep of that institution.

1906 and Stirling's finest—the Stirling Burgh Police Force—pose for this photograph taken at the time of their annual inspection. At this period the police station for the Burgh Police was in the Tolbooth where if one goes now the legend 'Police Office' can still be seen. Go now, as the local authority, having obtained some left over 'Fool's Gold' paint from Historic Scotland's 'restoration' in Stirling Castle are proposing painting the original random rubble and dressed ashlar. At the time of writing there are two trial panels on this fine eighteenth and nineteenth century building. One is just paint and other is, horror of horrors, plastered smooth with artificial stone lines scribed on. The board of the Disney Corporation would be proud of them.

The police office moved to a new station and District Court building in Spittal Street in 1934 and is now, of course, on the outskirts of town on the site of the demolished Clifford Park and Randolphfield mansions.

Five

A Stirling Miscellany

reathes there the man with soul so dead,
    Who never to himself hath said,
This is my own, my native land!
Whose heart hath ne'er within him burn'd,
As home his footsteps he hath turn'd,
    From wandering on a foreign strand!

Scott.

A once-familiar sight on the streets of Stirling were droves of cattle and sheep either being driven to market within the town (Burghmuir, on the site of the telephone exchange and Thistle Centre or in the Viewfield Place to Wallace Street area) or as droves on the way to large trysts or markets at Larbert from the Highlands and Islands. This mixed bunch are walking along Victoria Road on the edge of the King's Park.

Port Street, Stirling.

Some things do not change. This not so busy scene in Port Street shows one of these although not so easily done nowadays as here. Note the two men having a chat in the roadway. How often have you seen today's pedestrians dodging traffic or even greeting each other in the middle of Port Street? These two have a better chance. The tram heading for the terminus at St Ninians can not reach them and will be stopping soon to add on the trace horse to help the team pull it as far as Woodlands. The horse and cart is out close to the tramlines and, anyway, the driver, if he was like many other carters, would have a choice of repertoire in which to ask the gentlemen to step aside and a solitary cyclist can obviously take them on the inside. Today the left hand side would be filled with vehicles whose drivers had no real need to stop there causing obstruction up St Ninians Road, up the Allanpark and down the Wellgreen Road and at peak times, well beyond. Today, at almost anytime of day or evening the two way traffic fills the street almost non-stop. These are the things, which have changed. 'For the better'.

HUGH GAVIN & SONS,

GENERAL DRAPERS AND OUTFITTERS,

An Autumn day, c.1910.

One of Stirling's landmarks for a century and a half has been the Black Boy Fountain, although anatomically this figure is neither boy nor even a girl. It was bought from the Neilson Foundry in Glasgow by local residents. The Town Council of the day gave over the three cornered area of ground which was common ground anyway and the area was landscaped. Originally called the Gallows Mailing this area between the St Ninians Road and the Cambusbarron Road had, in former times, been the scene of public executions. Indeed the last time that human remains were found in this area was in 1924 when Central Scotland Motors Ltd were building their new garage at the corner of Allan Park and Port Street. Later this garage became the showrooms for Rossleigh Ltd and has now gone.

After lying dry for a number of years the fountain was renovated a few years ago and the water supply 'restored'. The present day trickle is an insult to the townspeople and is certainly nothing like the effect seen in the days before the 1975 re-organisation of local government, which allowed faceless, nameless beaurocracy to take command of our town's appearance and destiny.

In the 1860s there was a personality clash between the Revd Steedman at the Holy Rude Church and his assistant, Revd John T. Cowanlock. The latter went off to form his own congregation and build his own church. The ground chosen was in Dumbarton Road a piece of ground known at one point as Busbie's Orchard but at that time called Gibb's Garden as it had been used by the Gibb family to supply vegetables to their hotel, The Golden Lion, in King Street. This part of the sloping ground of the Back Walk is on the edge of a former bog called Bennie's Bog which stretches from Allanpark through Glebe Avenue to Victoria Square and gave some concern to the congregation and later, during a nine month renovation and extension during 1954, the upper part of the spire was removed to lessen the chance of the structure slipping. The first service was held in the renovated church on 30 January 1955. In 1935, the congregation had their premises extended by the addition of a new hall which was opened by Mrs Lawson of Castleview on 2 March.

ROBERT ADAM & SON, Glass and China Merchants, STIRLING.

Telephone No. 71.

Telegrams: "Adam, China, Stirling."

ONE OF THE SHOWROOMS.

The unveiling of Provost David Bayne's clock in Wallace Street in 1910. He also gifted the statue of Robert Burns in Dumbarton Road to the town in 1914.

This band of workers are the masons and others employed on building the Municipal Buildings in the Corn Exchange. In 1907-1908 the council instituted an open competition judged by the well known architect, William Leiper and fifty-nine sets of plans were sent in. First prize was awarded to Salmon & Son and Gillespie of Glasgow. Cost was estimated to be £12,000 exclusive of the value of the site. One alternative to the Corn Exchange site was a building proposed by Ebenezer Simpson, a local architect which could be built cheaper. This would have stood between Spittal Street and Baker Street on the site now occupied by the 1960s concrete and glass monstrosity occupied by the *Press and Journal* and Inland Revenue, etc. The council of the day actually asked the ratepayers to approve the building costs and organized a ballot in 1910. The way finances were worked it was claimed that, whatever site and building was chosen, there would be no cost to the ratepayers. The Corn Exchange design and site was picked and, although disagreement was to continue, Stirling got a fine municipal building albeit it was only two-thirds built. It was, however, to be ruined by the extension opened in 1966. This is a double blow in that original plans to complete a symmetrical design still existed and the original architect's practice was still operating, albeit under a different name. The concept of asking those who pay the salaries and expenses of the current council before committing large sums of money on various high profile schemes is something that is entirely foreign to today's councillors and officials. Note the two or three young fellows in the photograph, especially the one fourth from the right in the second row from the front. His 'doo lichter bunnet' would keep his shoulders dry in a downpour. Note also the number of collars and ties worn by the tradesmen. What a difference from today's 'bricklayer's bum'.

More of Stirling's heritage meets the bulldozer.